# ROSA BRANSON
## A PORTRAIT

Lynn Michell

¶

Published by Linen Press, London 2021

8 Maltings Lodge

Corney Reach Way

London W4 2TT

www.linen-press.com

Cover art: Michael Shpakov
www.michaelshpakov.co.uk

Photographs by Michael Shpakov and Lynn Michell

Typeset by The Press Gang
www.press-gang.co.uk

Printed and bound by Lightning Source

ISBN 978-1-8380603-5-0

# About the author

LYNN WRITES – has always written – and runs Linen Press, a small indie publishing house for women writers: www. linen-press.com. It's a fine balancing act but ever since she watched Elvira Madigan, she's secretly wanted to be a tightrope walker.

Her fifteen books are published by HarperCollins, Longman and The Women's Press. They include a six-book, illustrated writing scheme for primary schools, and *Shattered*, a book based on interviews with thirty people with severe Chronic Fatigue Syndrome. She and her two sons were badly affected and lived in the ME Ghetto for too many years.

Two books are close to her heart. Her debut novel, *White Lies*, runner-up for the Robert Louis Stevenson Award, is about an adulterous affair between a soldier's wife and an intelligence officer who understands Africa, played out against the backdrop of Kenya during the 1950s Mau Mau uprising. *The Red Beach Hut* tells the story of a fine but fated friendship between two outsiders, a man and a boy, on a windswept English beach. It is about belonging and bigotry.

When not writing or editing, for the past ten years Lynn has been building a house and landscaping a rocky plot of land in an oak forest high above a small village in southern France. Hands on.

Find the author on her website:

https://lynnmichellauthor0.webnode.com

# Other books by Lynn Michell

# Reviews

'Very inspiring. You are a wonderful writer. I am just an automatic paintbrush.'

— Rosa Branson, 2020

'I was knocked out by your description of being in the house with Rosa. It is brilliant and absorbing, immediate and atmospheric. It hooks the reader into wanting to get to know this extraordinary woman. The Rosa chapters are magic! Such beautiful writing and scene setting. This is a wonderful way to tell a life, a wonderful way to bring Rosa to life. If my life was to be told, this is the way I'd want it done!'

— Avril Joy, winner of the Costa and People's Prize, author of
*Millie and Bird, Sometimes a River Song* and *Going in with Flowers*
www.avriljoy.com

'Over the many years I've known her, Rosa has talked about her life in bite-size pieces. To read the whole story is wonderful and rings absolutely true. The vignettes of scenes throughout Rosa's fascinating life are tantalising with her own words woven through. We hear Rosa's inimitable voice. This wonderful book captures Rosa's great strength of character, her unquenchable passion to promote classical painting, her astonishing talent and her enormous generosity. It is a 'must read' for any aspiring artist and for anyone with ambitious dreams to fulfil.'

— Heath Rosselli, Honorary Freeman of the Worshipful Company of
Painter-Stainers and co-founder of The Worlington Movement
www.rosabransonandtheworlingtonmovement.com

'A compelling and deeply felt portrait of an artist who deserves to be better known. Lynn Michell has written a narrative which has the intimacy and power of memoir.'

— Ali Bacon, author of *In the Blink of an Eye* and *A Kettle of Fish*
www.alibacon.wordpress.com

# Contents

# Now

# Foreword
# Heath Rosselli

## 'THERE'S NO SUCH WORD AS CAN'T!'

ROSA'S WORDS RING in my ears every time I stumble upon a seemingly impossible part of a painting that I can't find my way around. As Rosa's protégées, we artists who have been lucky enough to come under her wing at some stage in our painting career know those familiar words all too well, and we hear Rosa's insistent voice resounding in our heads!

For many of us aspiring painters, Rosa has been a saviour and has kept us painting when we have been tempted to throw in the towel and give up altogether. As traditionalists, we have been going against the grain of current fashion for many decades as you will read in this extraordinary and wonderful account of Rosa's life and work.

Through this book, we have the opportunity to share and discover how Rosa's lifetime passion as a painter began, progressed, flourished and continues to bear wonderful fruit. We find out how this lifelong passion has punctuated a life that has been remarkable in so many other ways.

I look back to the time when I first met Rosa in 2000, just after I had broken my right arm quite badly. I was all ready to give up painting forever, but by one of those chance meetings that I strongly believe was 'meant to be'. Rosa came into my life like a fairy godmother and invited me to visit her studio. I had no idea who she was or what I should find there.

Like so many other despondent would-be artists arriving on her doorstep, I was absolutely stunned by the beautiful paintings that fill the house in Highgate and by her uncommon warmth as she invited me into her world. It quickly became clear that Rosa's universe is unlike anywhere else. There is something quite magical about that house on the hill in leafy Highgate where London is left outside and you enter Rosa's realm. It is a place of both unbreakable optimism and steely determination, where women support women, artists support artists, and where anyone with an open heart and mind will be given a warm welcome at the front door. Quite possibly, they may find their path changed forever – just as mine was that day.

On that first visit, Rosa suggested that I, like many others, come to her studio once a week with whatever commission I was working on, and she would advise and encourage. In all the years of painting with Rosa, soaking up her fount of knowledge and invaluable advice, she has never asked for anything in return other than a determination to keep painting. She completely understands the struggle we endure as artists who haven't been taught the traditional painting methods of the Old Masters. I now consider myself rather fortunate that I didn't attend art school, where these techniques are actively discouraged.

Since then, I have met many of Rosa's young students and heard similar stories. One young American called Amy turned up on my doorstep in 2003, having been to art school for four years in Washington State and learned little. She had been trying to teach art in Germany when she was sent to me by a sympathetic friend who knew that I painted in the Renaissance style. Amy had planned to stay over a weekend to work alongside me and pick up some knowledge, but ended up staying six months, working rather like an apprentice in the studio. She came with me on my weekly visits to Rosa, and then moved in with Rosa for a year before going on to successfully paint and teach near Seattle.

Amy is just one of a succession of young artists from all over the world given board and lodging as well as tuition by 'Mother Hen Rosa'. She has taken so many of us under her wing over the years, not only changing despair into hope, but transforming our lives. It is amazing to think of the ripple effect Rosa has created in young painters from different generations who are dispersed across the globe, their potential unlocked and their confidence and hopes restored.

Aware of the many unknown painters out there who need this kind of help, and in the spirit of Rosa's passion for creating connections with young artists, Rosa and I co-founded The Worlington Movement, so called after the village in Suffolk where I live. This is an online platform where despairing artists can find like-minded souls as well as a gateway to Rosa herself. We continue to seek her advice and she continues to give it, freely and willingly.

The Worlington Movement has had several successful exhibitions since it was founded, but we are so geographically dispersed that collaborations are hard to organise. We are also very busy with our own work; painting in layers in the Renaissance manner is painstakingly slow which perhaps is why art schools don't want to know. Nor is this style of painting commercially viable... But then art and commercialism don't always go hand in hand. The path to technical excellence in traditional oil painting is a very lonely one, as Rosa discovered as a young girl, so it is vital to stick together and support one another. We are not in competition with each other; we are kindred spirits within an artistic minority.

Meanwhile, well into her late eighties, Rosa continues to stun us with her incredible talent, painting with a technical brilliance that few of us will ever achieve. She lives her life with the vigour, optimism and confidence that have come to define her. This is illustrated by her extensive travels to research her charity paintings. For Help the Aged, she went to India. For The Salvation Army paintings, she travelled to Kenya, Zimbabwe, Korea, Hong Kong, Bolivia, Haiti, Dallas, Portugal and Switzerland. For Mercy Ships in 2007 she went to the poorest parts of Sierra Leone and Liberia and spent time on the hospital ships watching the doctors perform vital operations on the poorest of the poor.

Rosa's astonishing work ethic is something to behold, motivating her to work for five hours every day without exception, and with two fierce aims: that her paintings raise awareness and funding for the charities dear to her heart, and that fledgling artists flourish as they make their way in the art world with everything that she has passed on to them. She never sells her work nor charges for her tuition. She continues to paint and she continues to give. Her altruism knows no bounds.

How can we repay Rosa? We can carry the baton and pass it on to the next generation, ensuring that her precious legacy lives on and that the increasingly elusive skills used and taught by her are not lost forever. It is Rosa's fervent wish that her story, captured so beautifully within these pages, will inspire and encourage artists – and indeed any lost artistic souls – who are lucky enough to find and read it.

I am happy to have this opportunity to thank Rosa on behalf of all of us in the art world who owe her so much.

See www.rosabransonandtheworlingtonmovement.com

# About this biography

I'D LIKE TO give you a few stepping stones before you make your way into this story of Rosa Branson's life so that the journey is smooth and you do not trip unnecessarily. You may expect a conventional biography, but this isn't one. I have not stepped back and told Rosa's story at arm's length by collecting facts then presenting them in the third person: 'Rosa hated Camberwell Art College and became depressed because the Impressionist style taught there was completely wrong for her.' Most of her story is written in vignettes, like chapters in a novel with Rosa as the central character. I stay with her own emphasis on what is important, pivotal and of lasting influence: her determination to paint in a style that is unfashionable but absolutely right for her, her reverence and love for her parents and their communist principles, and her commitment to truth and integrity in her long life. As far as I can, I have slipped into Rosa's skin and I look through her eyes. I use her own words throughout the book, marked in italics. Rosa speaks for herself.

This is the story Rosa needs to tell herself. There are a few places where the dates and ages Rosa cites do not quite match up with chronologies recorded elsewhere. These tensions and inconsistencies are part of the telling of her story and are interesting and revealing in themselves. They are a natural part of autobiographical memory.

Between the fictionalised scenes are a few verbatim extracts from our conversations where my voice and Rosa's alternate. I use these to bring into sharp focus the big signposts in her life, in particular the death of her father, Clive Branson, when she is ten.

I don't plunge straight into the past. I give a brief explanation of the technique used by the Old Masters which is central to Rosa's story. I also describe my first meeting with Rosa in 2017 and my indelible impressions of an extraordinary woman. On that first visit, Rosa showed me round the house in which she has lived since 1955 and which is a backdrop to our conversations and to her story.

I have taken liberties with structure and style and have included verbatim extracts from our conversations. Through these different texts, the leitmotifs that shape Rosa's life remain constant and enduring. I would love to think that this is the autobiography that Rosa might have written if her métier had been words not images.

# I Introduction to the technique of the Old Masters

# The technique

THERE ARE SEVERAL leitmotifs that shine through this biography but the light from one is pervasive, steady and fierce. When Rosa discusses and reflects on the way she paints, using the technique of the Old Masters, her eyes light up and her voice is awash with certainty and passion. She refers to a method of painting in oils, closely based on that used during the Renaissance, which emerged as a distinct style in Italy in about 1400, and the Baroque, which flourished in Europe from the early 17th to the mid-18th century. It consists of the painstaking building of layer upon layer over the whole canvas, the composition established whole but shadowy in the first layer of raw sienna. It follows a prescribed sequence and uses the correct mixes of washes and colours. Rosa was never taught this technique but longed to learn it because she was convinced that it was the only way she could accurately and faithfully paint the modern world. But at Camberwell Art College and at the Slade School of Art, her tutors were dismissive, even contemptuous of this style and were incredulous that Rosa wanted to travel backwards to adopt such an old-fashioned method. Students were taught impressionistic styles of painting and were expected to adopt and practise only those. Again and again, with scorn and loathing, Rosa describes the Cézanne-influenced *spots and daubs and blobs* which she had to throw at her canvases. Her rejection is adamant. Her despair, palpable.

I describe the technique briefly here, before I tell her story, because it is central to the choices she makes, to the blocks and challenges she encounters, and the paths she chooses as she equips herself single-mindedly and courageously with the skills she needs to become a very particular kind of painter, one that long ago went out of fashion and is no longer taught in art colleges. For Rosa, there is no alternative. This is her idée fixe. Her passion.

This is no sudden revelation, but rather a slow-burning certainty that stretches back to her childhood before it gathers its momentum into the future. Between the ages of four and six, for one very brief period, perhaps idealised in retrospect, she lives happily at home with both parents, Noreen and Clive Branson. She watches her adored father paint the portraits of Battersea's working classes and the dreadful conditions in which they work and live. We can imagine the animated conversations about painting and politics as the little girl, an only child, stands at her father's side at his easel, watching him layer his oils onto the canvas while he explains what he is doing and why. And we can be certain of the animated talk afterwards, when father, mother and daughter gather round the kitchen table to pick over their day's work. The values of Rosa's parents are played out in every move they make: towards their daughter, towards other people, and in the way they live their lives. Those values are non-negotiable: integrity, truth, commitment, compassion, passion. Rosa soaks it up into the fibre of her being where it is lodged for the rest of her long life.

At the age of six, Rosa is taken by her mother to the National Gallery and shown the paintings loved and revered by Clive.

'Your daddy says this artist is the greatest in the world,' Noreen tells her.

I looked up at the wonderful paintings by Botticelli and Titian and Leonardo and I thought, 'When I grow up I will do pictures like this.'

The impact of seeing those great paintings for the first time, and hearing her mother say how much her father adores them, is profound. Imprinted by this experience, Rosa carries it into the years ahead as she commits to achieving her often thwarted ambition of painting properly.

# SEQUENCE OF THE PAINTING:
# MEETING HENRY IN HEAVEN

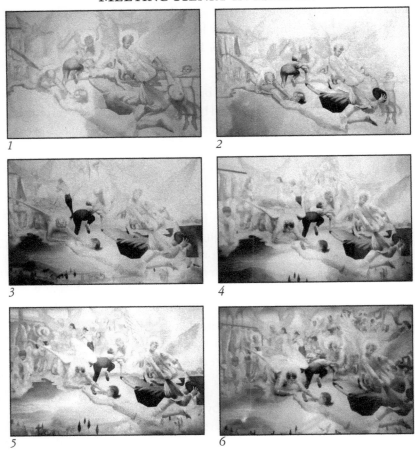

*The progression of a painting using the technique of the Old Masters*

13

She is determined that she must and will master the technique used by these giants of a bygone era. *My ambition was to paint the contemporary world with the same techniques as the great Renaissance painters.* This thread, strong and unbroken, is woven through the fabric of Rosa's life.

Rosa not only explains how she uses the technique but shows me. She has several books of photographs showing the progression of a painting from the first raw sienna shadowy outline through to the final stage where all the colour and detail are added. I ask her to talk me through one of her paintings, step by step, as if I know nothing about the technique, and this is what she says as she turns the pages that show a painting in progress. The composition, whole and in detail, is ready to download from her imagination before she starts and before she transfers it to the canvas, a pale but complete skeleton created with the first layer of raw sienna.

*It's a canvas. So you start to draw in the bits that you want in the right place.*

In what colour?

*Well, it's raw sienna, and because it's raw sienna it doesn't interfere with the colours.*

Why?

*Because it's not too dark. Then gradually you put the light in.*

When you start a painting do you have it complete in your imagination?

*In general, yes.*

So when you come to do the first layers you know where you're going.

*Yes, I do.*

And you know what you're working towards.

*That's right.*

Right down to the fine detail.

*Yes, that's right.*

How do you envisage it? Can you see it?

*I've got a funny head! I do. I see it.*

You have a way of looking...

*Yes, that's not normal.*

Does it ever change? In the process of painting?

*The first idea with the charity painting[1] is that the sunlight is in the middle and it radiates out.*

Why do you put sunlight in the middle?

*To give a feeling of optimism.*

But painting isn't only about technique, Rosa explains. *If you have real feelings without the technique or the technique without real feelings you haven't got good art. It's got to be both.* Rosa talks often about the visions which accompany her throughout her life, and how important and necessary they are for her paintings. When she is pregnant, the visions vanish and she panics, but they return after giving birth, and Rosa can again take inspiration from them. She also explains how she translates anger into painting, sometimes literally by painting someone who has behaved badly towards her as an evil creature. That way, the negative emotions are transformed and dissipated. During times of deep sorrow, Rosa transposes her grief into compositions. *I have learnt that when life is comfortable one paints comfortable pictures, but when life hits you badly, you come up with your best work. When Henry was dying, I created a painting of us meeting in heaven. It was eight foot by five foot and expressed exactly what I was feeling. It took nine months to complete.*

A more detailed description of the technique, based on an interview with Francesca Maxwell, can be found in the Appendix.

www.rwa.org.uk/artists/francesca-berlingieri-maxwell

---

1. Rosa Branson refers here to the large storyboard canvases painted at the request of charities and lobby groups, both for display and to support fundraising. She has painted for charities for the past twenty years.

# 2 THE HOUSE

# The Highgate house
# 2017

IT'S A STEEP climb from the Airbnb flat on Archway Road up into Highgate. Traffic roars along this hectic arterial road. The blustery wind blows rubbish around my feet and grit into my eyes. It takes a while to get a long enough gap in the traffic to make a break for the other side. I turn into Southwood Lane and start to climb again, but almost at once I'm in different territory. It's a quiet road that bends upwards, lined with mature trees, and with detached houses set back in well tended gardens. Wisteria, jasmine and clematis spill over fences, scenting the autumn air.

Rosa's large house is at the very top, painted white and covered in scaffolding. The front garden is not manicured and its flowers and weeds bloom in wild clumps. Overgrown shrubs lean across the front door and roses make their way to the huge bay window. I ring the bell. Rosa opens it and stands with her hand on the jamb, a soft smile making me feel immediately welcome. She's wearing thick tights, a warm skirt and a patterned woollen jumper, and has a small smear of green paint on one cheek. Where others might rush forward with nervous first words and gestures, Rosa stays exactly where she is and exudes a quiet calm and a sense of belonging. Or is her mind simply elsewhere, still on the vast unfinished charity painting I will later see in her studio? She talks about the scaffolding, without any introductions or social niceties, as if she has known me for ages. I sense that I'm with someone who is unusually and completely comfortable in her own skin, in her own house, in her own routine, in her own life; someone who will welcome whoever arrives on her doorstep, perhaps after a brief and almost invisible appraisal. She stands like a strong-rooted plant and looks me briefly up and down, then tells me to come in and kisses me like an old friend. She smells of wool and paint. Glancing back at the scaffolding, she continues her saga about some scam with cowboy workmen and roof repairs which cost her dear, but it's all sorted now, and she seems unbothered by any of it. She closes the door, the scaffolding forgotten. I am relaxed. My breathing has slowed. In this woman's presence, I have no need of any social mask. I too can be myself. She exudes a quiet generosity and acceptance.

My first impression is of a house whose decor hasn't changed in decades. In the hall, on the Edwardian marble floor with its mosaic pattern, is a wooden stand for umbrellas and a row of pegs for coats. The walls are thick-papered and a light dangles from the ceiling in a simple old-fashioned shade. A staircase rises to upper floors. My second impression is of art everywhere, of framed paintings in the hall and on the walls on either side of the stairs, with glimpses of many more, some huge, on the first landing. All of it will be viewed later. Rosa opens a door on the left and leads me into the front room whose rose-crowded bay window I could see from outside. She makes me feel as if I come here often. I sense in Rosa a calm wisdom as well as a gentle irony, as if she views the world as somewhat absurd. Later, this first impression will play out as pretty much correct. Rosa lives to paint, and while she continues to offer support – artistic and personal – to the students who come and stay for a day or a week or a year, and although she talks proudly and warmly about her family, I think that she sees the world only as a blurry backdrop to her art. She doesn't focus on it except to paint it.

Rosa's living room is a surprise. For a start, there's only one place to sit and apart from an old bureau, there's almost no furniture. On three sides, enormous paintings are propped up, five and six deep, facing out, separated and protected by white sheets, and reaching two-thirds of the way up the walls. Outside the bay window, roses sway against the glass and the bright sun moves in and out of clouds, colouring the room in dazzling light then dimming it again. In that window is a sofa covered in apricot coloured bed sheets. We sink into it, squashed together. I feel somewhat overwhelmed by the charity paintings which are surreal, busy, and crammed with dozens and dozens of portraits of people who look out from backdrops of blue skies and white clouds and exotic cities and landscapes. The colours are alive and vivid. The detail is astonishing. At first, my eyes flick over the paintings on either side of us, as Rosa explains which charity commissioned which, and names the people whose portraits she has included as stand-ins for people from across the world who cannot pose for her. 'That's my hairdresser and that's my grocer and that's a neighbour.' In her memoir, she writes; 'My daughter was queueing for vegetables in the shop, saw the greengrocer and said loudly, 'You're Jesus!' to the amusement of the other people in the queue. They were stars in many of my paintings.'

But even with the visual competition from the charity storyboards, there's one painting that dominates this room. Standing alone, not in a stack but propped up and facing us, bathed in direct light from the window, is a painting that is utterly compelling. Its clarity and drama demand that your gaze returns to it again and again. Rosa explains that it's a painting of life and death. She says that it depicts the death of her beloved father, Clive Branson, in action in Burma when she was ten years old. The ration book lying at the bottom is an exact replica of her father's and the scattered sheet music is copied note for note from genuine sheets of music from that era. When she leaves the room on some pretext – and in retrospect I wonder if it's to hide her emotions – I jump up and stand close to the painting, my gaze drawn down to the bottom third. The detail is incredibly sharp: on the sheet music, in the print on the crumpled but legible newspapers with their headlines about war, in the skull wearing a helmet, in the medal and the ration book that was found on Clive's body. It is photographically realistic but also surreal, and it is upsetting, as a painting of death and a shrine to Rosa's father has to be upsetting. This room is more a gallery than a living room. In the evenings, Rosa sits upstairs, not here, but I wonder what she feels when she does sit on the sofa and is brought back to the moment of her father's death. I'm still standing by the painting when Rosa comes back, and she

*War and Peace*

*War and Peace – lower half of painting*

briefly answers a couple of questions, but from the expression in her eyes and the tremor in her voice, I understand that her father's death, seventy-four years previously, is not a subject to throw into a first conversation with an unknown woman who has turned up to write her life story. Later, she will tell me a lot more.

Perhaps to smooth over a troubled moment, she offers to show me round the rest of the house. Next door is her large, paint-splashed studio which overlooks the long, untidy garden and is lit from the north with the light beloved of painters. This is where Rosa paints for seven hours every day, never taking a day off unless 'it's in my diary'. A day without painting is marked like an official holiday. In this room, Rosa has painted through marriages with Alan Hopkins and Henry Hooper, and during a loving relationship with Harold Sumption.

In the middle of the room, propped on a large easel with a stool positioned in front, is an eight foot by five foot storyboard painting for the Red Cross in an early stage of completion. I have to step carefully past a wide set of artists' drawers housing paper and paintings to reach it. Above it is a pulley which Rosa uses to manoeuvre the canvas up, down and sideways so that she can reach the part she is working on. Because she paints minute, exact, photographic detail, she needs to be very close to the canvas. I'm fortunate to see this painting today because all she has done so far is apply the first layer, the raw sienna, which sketches the whole composition but doesn't include colour or highlights or details. This is the scaffolding of the painting, like that outside which holds up the house. We can see the whole composition in a pale ochre-brown which is understated and flat. Almost like a photographic negative. Later this under painting will be covered, layer by exact layer. Of course, the visible raw sienna prompts Rosa to talk at length about a subject dear to her heart and absolutely central to her painting style – the five layers used by the Old Masters and learned despite, not because of art college, over many years of copying and studying and copying again. About this, I will hear much, much more. For now though, I stop staring at the painting, listen to Rosa, and take in the rest of the room. Above the easel is a long shelf that holds maybe six or seven enormous glass jars crammed with paintbrushes. Flat, round, thin, thick, pointed sable tips with wooden handles fight for space. Rosa's implements are beautiful, lined up in a row, waiting to be chosen and put to work. How does she know which one to pick?

It's only now that I notice another person in the room, her back to us, silently working on a painting in a corner, near the window. She's been very still and I've been so absorbed in the painting, and the room with its tools of the trade and materials, I didn't see her, nor has Rosa mentioned her because, I find out later, students painting in corners of the house are part of the set-up here and need no introduction. The young painter says hello and carries on copying a skull and pearl necklace on crushed fabric. She is one of a revolving door of students who turn up on Rosa's doorstep after finding out about her on the grapevine, and are taken in, for days or weeks or months because they are troubled and lost and depressed, blocked in their desire to paint, and utterly demoralised by a style of teaching that has extinguished, not nurtured, their creativity. Rosa recognises in them her younger self at Camberwell, in despair throughout her three years there, and suicidal at one point because she knew that she did not want to paint in the impressionistic style taught there. Rosa doesn't teach the students, but provides space and security, an insight into a painter's way of life, an immersion in art, and answers to their questions only if they ask. Some discover themselves and their talent under her roof. A few don't.

The dining room, next door to the studio with its window similarly facing the garden, seems at first to have some alternative source of light because the entire room glows with a honey-gold radiance. It felt cold in the north light of the studio but here there is tangible warmth. I look for hidden spotlights but the radiance seems to pour from the paintings on all the walls surrounding the table. These are the paintings Rosa completed during her second, very happy marriage to Henry Hooper, after he asked why she didn't paint beautiful objects like candles and fruit. He had made the suggestion tactfully after he found her painting yet another skull and mushrooms on black velvet. And so she painted a bowl of oranges lit by candlelight, and carried on painting fruit and pewter plates and sparkling jewellery and musical instruments gilded by flickering light. These rich, glowing paintings reflect the warmth and joy of her marriage. The apricot and orange tones from the paintings spill onto the polished wood of the table, burnishing it. The whole room is alive with colour. If rooms have emotions, this one remembers a shared happiness. Here, I would be content to sit down and sip a glass of wine, soothed by the terracotta glow.

Facing the back garden is a galley kitchen where two people can't pass without a crush. The old, free-standing units are mismatched, the sink and stove ancient, the shelves bending under the weight of pots, pans and containers. It's not an attractive space, and there's been no attempt to modernise it. Later Rosa will tell me that during her first marriage when she and Alan Hopkins were young and engrossed in painting, she didn't cook. They ate fish and chips and anything else that was fast and simple. It was only after she married Henry Hooper, and he gently asked why she didn't cook proper meals, that she applied herself to acquiring this new skill. Once she had tested her recipes on Henry, and gained his approval, she devoted one weekend a month to the planning, buying and cooking of dishes for a dinner party for Highgate friends at which she displayed her new talent. There are inescapable parallels here between Rosa's acquisition of skills for painting and for cooking. For her, it is always about technique. She says she became a very good cook.

We retrace our footsteps and climb the stairs to the first floor landing which is dominated by an enormous, powerful painting of a tiger striding through the jungle. There is a sober, almost severe portrait of Noreen, and Clive Branson's portrait of Kalkar. More an exhibition area than a landing on the way to the upper and lower floors, I need to pause here to appreciate the beauty that circles the space. There are too many paintings to take in on this first visit, but Rosa points out a beautiful portrait of her daughter, Peggy, and tells me she is a famous interior designer.

This house is as much an art gallery as a home, halted in time, but it is comfortable and unpretentious. I wonder if anything has been changed since the three-generation family converged here in 1955. There's faded, patterned wallpaper from that era, swirly carpets, and dark, bulky furniture. No-one has attempted a Grand Designs refurbishment here.

Rosa's bedroom is at the back, overlooking the garden, and so crammed that it is difficult to fit two of us in, let alone move around once inside. There's a high double bed covered in a silky maroon quilt, a tall wardrobe and chests of drawers. Every surface is crowded with a jumbled mix of art and necessity, a marble egg next to a plastic alarm clock, and a multitude of framed photographs. The mantlepiece holds china cups given to her by her daughter. How can she dust all of this, I wonder? The walls are crowded with Rosa's art. I stop dead in front of a fabric collage which hangs just inside the door. Rosa explains it is one of only two embroideries in her possession from the period when she sewed rather than painted, when her children were small and she didn't want to poison them with paint. For seven years, during the day, she exchanged a brush for a needle and stitched intricate fabric collages. This one is dark, heavily detailed and exquisite, a picture of creatures and flowers created by the tiniest stitches. In the black fabric sky are pinprick silver stars. I ask where all the other embroideries are and she says she doesn't know. Maybe she gave them away. Maybe she sold them. She shrugs her shoulders in dismissal. Later, she will show me the second, larger collage on the landing and I feel bereft that only two out of hundreds remain. The bedroom walls are hung with portraits of her late husband, Henry Hooper, her son, Michael, and herself when young. 'That's a…' she names a well known artist, deadpan, waving her hand at one of the paintings. As we turn to leave the room, Rosa points to a big ceramic jar on top of the wardrobe. 'Crystals,' she explains. 'We were all getting terrible headaches from the electricity cables so we consulted someone who told us to place crystals in every room to neutralise the radio waves. The headaches have gone.'

Rosa moves on and opens the door to what was, in the original layout of the house, the biggest bedroom above the living room, with another bay window looking over the front. When Noreen bought the house in 1955 for the whole family – Rosa, her husband Alan Hopkins, their baby Peggy Ann, and herself – she converted this room into her sitting room where she also worked for much of the day. The big, round table is the one where she sat every morning, her typing starting up as regularly as an alarm clock and echoing downstairs where Rosa was either sewing or sketching. Light streams in the window. A small TV is tucked into one dark corner with a single armchair nearby. Rosa tells me she listens to the radio first thing in the morning before she starts painting and while she eats breakfast, and watches TV in the evenings. She has no computer or mobile phone. The walls in this room, like the walls everywhere, are covered with framed paintings but these are not Rosa's. The frames are older, the paintings somewhat yellowed by the light. They are darker than Rosa's paintings with heavy tones of brown, dark greens and reds. There are portraits of workers with lined, exhausted, dirt-smeared faces and scenes of people labouring in Battersea or caught in the Blitz. Of course. These are Clive Branson's paintings, hung here as if in a gallery dedicated to him. When I ask for confirmation, Rosa replies, her voice catching, 'Yes. These are Daddy's paintings.' Six of Clive's paintings hang in the Tate. I count forty-one on the walls in this room.

I think again about Clive's lasting legacy and his physical presence in this house that was once the family home. Downstairs is the huge painting that is both a shrine to her father and a portrait of a soldier killed in battle. Each time Rosa looks at the faithfully reproduced realism of his ration book and his helmet, she relives the moment of his death. I wonder if, after all the years, the emotions are calmed and blunted or if she wants to keep alive the shock of his going. In the evenings, Rosa sits in this upstairs gallery, watching the small television, her back to the wealth of her father's strong, passionate paintings. Each time she turns away from the screen, she sees his work. He is there with her – in his recognisable style, in the politics of his art, in his commitment to his ideals.

Rosa talks about the family portraits as we head back down the stairs to the ground floor and on down another flight to the basement which stretches underneath the whole house. It's quite dark and quite cold. No mod cons for this artisan section of the enterprise. The big wide space has a low ceiling. It's a rough and ready workroom dominated by a vast work table where Rosa does her own framing. On the floor, stacked on a trolley, in sets of drawers lined up against the walls and hung on the walls are the tools of the trade for framing and packing the paintings – wood, rolls of bubble wrap, stacks of brown paper, scissors, hammers, pliers and nails. There's too much to take in, and Rosa is rummaging through one stack of paintings which lean against the wall, showing me one after another and telling me about them. In a corner, another student paints bright cubes of colour. Like the one upstairs, she turns to say hello, then carries on with her work. Visitors, apparently, are expected to accept these students as an ordinary part of the set-up, not quite furniture, but an integral part of the house. In a filing cabinet, in old flimsy Kodak wallets, I discover four hundred and three photos of Rosa's paintings.

From this workspace, a door opens surprisingly into a small comfortable sitting room with a small chintz sofa, bookshelves heavy with folders, ring binders, books, photos and treasured artefacts, and a view of the garden. 'It's a place to put stuff. When I finish a little painting, it goes down here until it's collected,' Rosa tells me. In this room, once again, history is meticulously organised and stored. On one side of the fireplace are large ring binders containing photographs of all of Rosa's charity paintings and information about them being commissioned and revealed. On the other side are albums of the family, Rosa's personal history, dating back to her grandparents and forwards to her grandchildren. There is a photograph of four generations of Branson women – Noreen, Rosa, her daughter, Peggy, and her granddaughter. There are photos of Henry Hooper, but none of her first husband, Alan Hopkins.

This house has seen some transitions. It was bought by Noreen to be a family home because two young painters, Rosa and her husband, Alan Hopkins, lived in rented rooms and could not afford to purchase their own place. For six years, the young couple and their two young children spent most of their days downstairs while Noreen lived on the first floor with her own space to work. From Rosa's memoir and from what she tells me, there was an easy flow of movement up and down, though no doubt with well-established boundaries so that Noreen wasn't disturbed while she wrote her books, pamphlets and articles. Both an activist and a social historian, she worked with energy and commitment for the British Library Research Department from 1938 until her death in 2003, editing its magazine for twenty-eight years. It was at this table that she wrote her books on Britain in the 1920s and 1930s, on political activism in

East London, and her volumes on the history of the Communist Party. Rosa's children ran upstairs to spend an hour with their grandmother before they went to bed; she liked doing organised, practical activities with them like drawing, craft and reading. After the breakdown of Rosa's first marriage, and with Alan admitted to an asylum, the house became the base for two working women, one upstairs, one down, both putting in long hours with small children roaming between the floors. In 1971, Rosa married Henry Hooper and, simultaneously freed from bringing up young children and from financial worries, they travelled the world so that Rosa could paint exotic scenes in exotic places, often leaving Noreen alone here. Since 2003, when Noreen died, the house has been Rosa's home, studio and gallery, generously opened up to students who arrive in states of unrest and distress about their art, as she herself was at their age. There is one student who lives in the rooms on the top floor and others who come and go, adding their youth, energy, confusion and passion to the house of memories.

Rosa has lived in the house for sixty-two years.

*Rosa in her studio*

*Living room*

*Dining room*

*Mantlepiece with wood painted by Rosa to match wallpaper*

*Landing*

*Clive Branson's paintings*

*Noreen's sitting room*

*Rosa's bedroom*

*Basement*

*Basement storage room*

# 3 The death of Clive Branson

# The death of Clive Branson

**B**EHIND ROSA'S LIFELONG wish to *paint properly* lies one event of such profound emotional significance that it fuses with her young, still fragile hope of becoming *a proper painter* and solidifies into the formidable driving force behind her non-negotiable determination to be an artist who *paints the real world with the technique of the Old Masters.*

The death of her beloved father when she is ten years old, before he can fulfil his treasured promise to teach his little girl to paint, is almost impossible to bear. The trauma of losing him, and losing that cherished hope for her future, drops into place a series of stepping stones which Rosa follows as she sets out on her often lonely, lifelong journey to *paint properly.* Clive Branson is her guiding star. Her lodestone. Her inspiration.

He is frozen forever in time as the young father Rosa lived with for only two years, from the age of four to six, a time recorded in her memoir and spoken about in our interviews as utterly joyful: *Daddy was a lovely person. Lovely and very funny and a marvellous artist.* Her knowledge and her memories of him, treasured and stored during those precious years, come to a jarring halt when she is ten years old and he is killed in battle. Whether, after fifty-four years, she is still fulfilling that childlike wish to emulate and please her father by becoming a painter, or whether that lost promise mutates over the years into an absolute, rational conviction about painting in a particular style, we do not know. Nor does it matter. Throughout her own memoir and during the interviews, Rosa repeatedly acknowledges her unbroken allegiance to her father's memory and, when talking about him, slips easily into the skin of the ten-year-old child whose father was killed fighting in Burma in the Second World War.

*Now look...you asked what kind of a daddy did I have...this is the only letter I have from him and it's rather sweet* (she shows me a tiny letter written on a stamp). *He was a very kind man and this shows it. Very sweet. It's very powerful. It shows you the sort of daddy he was. And this was in his pocket when he was found dead. He was collecting stamps at that time so every time he wrote to my mother he wrote little things on extra stamps for me. So you see* _why_ *I paint in memory of him because he was such a kind man.*

Is he your inspiration?

*YES!*

Is he still here in spirit?

*YES! I do it in memory of Daddy, not to get famous or make money. I do it for Daddy.*

At the age of eighty-four, Rosa tells me, *I paint for Daddy.*

*Clive Branson*

*Clive, Rosa, Peggy and Michael*

*Clive Branson. Communist Demonstration*

*Clive Branson. 22nd July*

41

*Clive Branson. Noreen and Rosa*

*Clive Branson. Self-portrait*

# THEN

# 4 Before Rosa: Noreen Browne and Clive Branson

# April 1931
# Noreen is 20

A LL OF FASHIONABLE society has gathered here. The women pose in clinging evening gowns of chiffon, silk and satin. Cut on the bias, they create elegant, flowing lines and the hems swish across the floor when they wander from group to group, collecting envious or critical stares. Those who are bold and young wear the latest fashion of halternecks with plunging backs low enough to show a hint of a tantalising curve. The men are all the same. Their double-breasted dinner jackets and trousers are black with a stripe of stiff-pressed white wingtip shirt beneath, and a black or white butterfly bow tie.

The request goes round for people to take their seats in this large, lavishly furnished drawing room where heavy damask curtains shut out the remains of the darkening sky and hide the low shafts of amber light which gild tennis courts, croquet lawns, noble trees, landscaped parkland and, in the distance, a glassy lake. The house is a stage set to showcase the owners' wealth, the walls in this room alone displaying an art collection of formidable value.

Earlier in the day, housemaids and butlers pushed settees and fragile side tables against the wall and arranged the gilt trimmed chairs in a multi-layered semi-circle around the gleaming grand piano. Cigar smoke fogs the air. The polite buzz of conversation is broken by falsetto laughter

46

as girls, giddy with excitement at being newly 'out' respond coquettishly to the jokes and banter of men who know how to captivate and charm. After all, the code of conduct is fully understood. The young women are here to snare a husband, preferably one with a fortune, their mamas keeping a careful eye on proceedings while pretending to be engrossed in conversations about the latest recipes and their problems with staff. The season is in full swing. These evenings of lavish entertainment will continue, filling the idle hours of the idle rich as predictably as night follows day. Butlers in handsome new liveries weave in and out, bearing trays of fluted glasses filled with the best wines from the replete cellars. This audience, like many audiences in similar country houses, have persuaded themselves that they are here as do-gooders, giving up their precious time to contribute generously to the coffers of a charity chosen and sponsored by their hosts. They turn and turn about. Tomorrow brings another country home, another event for another charity. Or they gather simply for the fun of it, and to pass hours that can feel empty unless there are luncheons and dinners, opera and theatre, animal and husband hunting.

Noreen has come here not for the company, but to hear Fanny Davies, a professional pianist who performs on an equal footing with her male counterparts. It's considered a coup to have secured her for a mere charity event, albeit a grand one, and so the room is crammed and the audience is eager.

For Noreen, the event is bittersweet. Her thoughts, still raw, flick back to her end-of-year piano recital at the Guildhall School of Music. Her tutors had already concurred amongst themselves: Noreen Browne was musically gifted but lacked the necessary drive and ego to be a concert pianist. When the night arrived, and the hall was packed with relatives, friends, professional performers and influential people from the music industry, Noreen waited her turn, one of very few women amongst male performers, a bundle of nerves. Nevertheless she played her piece with technical precision. She thought her performance was probably adequate until afterwards her tutor had sidled up behind her seat and whispered in her ear.

'Such a shame, Noreen. Whatever came over you?'

Noreen turned to face the man who exuded disappointment.

'You don't know?' he asked.

No, she didn't know. She shook her head.

'You performed the entire piece an octave too high.'

'An octave too high?'

'Yes. You honestly don't know?'

No, she didn't, and she was mortified. And still she had to sit there, her cheeks burning, until the audience had risen and left, and the students, some glowing with hope and success, were free to go too. It was her only means of escape, albeit a slender one, and she might as well have kicked the open door shut without even trying to go through it.

Here, now, her failings are emphasised by the appearance of a woman who has made it to the top of her profession along a route that is now closed to her. While she sits fretting, those who know – and of course almost everyone knows – whisper that Noreen Browne's position is hardly a tragedy. After all, the most eligible bachelors are circling like hungry eagles. She will have her pick. Training to be a concert pianist was always an irrelevancy.

Noreen sighs, and shakes herself back to the present. And reality.

Squeezing into the last seat but one towards the back, she composes her features to discourage any approach, any empty chatter, any pre-prepared opening compliment. She ignores the young man who sits down beside her. Young men frequently seek her out, but in their slight conversation she feels nothing but contempt and yawning boredom. Nor does she bother to hide it. They, in turn, find her forward and outspoken, and are surprised at her blunt readiness to disagree with their half-formed opinions. Her wealth, however, is even more formidable, and so they foolishly persevere.

When she briefly turns her head, having appreciated his silence, she sees a fine looking man who looks straight ahead. From a rapid appraisal formed in that first glance, she concludes he is indifferent to the wide-eyed glances flung his way from the pretty young women keen to attract his attention. Perhaps like me he is not here to be seen, she wonders briefly, before removing her attention.

'Have you heard Fanny Davies play?' he asks, without preamble.

'No, have you?'

'Yes. I went to one of her lecture recitals.'

'Which composer?'

'Schumann. She played short passages to illustrate each of her points. One of her pupils played too. You know she funds a prize for talented players?'

'I didn't know that. I wonder who enters? Only those from these circles, I suppose.' Noreen scans the assembled rich with undisguised distaste.

'Probably. After all, the dice is loaded. How many working class parents can afford piano tuition for their daughters?'

Noreen turns her head and stares at this young man who has expressed an opinion, and one that echoes her own. He is handsome in a careless sort of way and she senses he moves outside the tight circles of class conventions. His presence is strong and charismatic, but without the self-satisfaction and ego of so many lesser others.

'I'm Clive Branson,' he says, offering her his hand. 'I know who you are.'

She has heard something of him in the tittle-tattle that she sometimes can't avoid. Upper class but trade. New money. Certainly not titled. Wasn't there some gossip about him turning his back on his wealthy family and making his own way?

'What do you do?' she asks.

'I've enrolled at the Slade. I intend to paint.'

Noreen allows herself a small smile of satisfaction at her, so far, correct supposition.

'You mean…as a hobby?'

'Good God, no! I want to be a painter. An artist. I don't normally attend…' his eyes narrow as they sweep across the room, '…events like this.'

'But your background…'

'Our wealth comes from banking. My father made our fortune. And yes, my parents are appalled that their son has announced that he will be an artist, not a banker or a soldier as suits his recently won place in society.'

'Lucky you! You can afford to be a painter,' Noreen continues, pursuing a troubling point. 'You don't have to earn your living. You'll have an allowance.'

'I reject all that,' he says firmly. 'I won't accept a penny from my family. I'll make my own way like other artists. I don't intend to dabble!'

Their intense exchange is brought to a halt by a burst of clapping as their host begs silence and gushes her introduction for their famous guest. Fanny Davies walks on to the stage and takes her place at the gleaming piano.

'I'd like to hear more,' Noreen whispers.

'After the concert, we can escape. There's a Lyons tea house nearby that's open all night. Unless you want to stay and mingle…'

'I do not,' Noreen replies, and secretly shivers in delight at the thought of such daring. They will slip out when people crowd into the dining room for refreshments. In the crush, no-one will notice. And who cares if they do?

Noreen has never set foot in a Lyons tea house and is all eager attention. The place is almost empty in these dark, early hours. A shift worker stares glumly at his cup of tea, perhaps reluctant to walk out and make his way to a cold, unwelcoming room in a cheap boarding house. Noreen and Clive lean in, cups of coffee long cold, oblivious to the few other customers who come and go. Until dawn breaks, they talk with steady passion and zeal, interrupt each other, finish each other's sentences, go over the same common ground. For both, there is astonishment and satisfaction in the echoes and ripples of the same sentiments, the same ideas that pass from one to the other. They speak of their consuming worry about a society that's in the grip of a terrible depression.

'It's a disaster for the working classes,' Clive says, impassioned. 'I have seen such abject poverty. The working classes are suffering ill health and early deaths. It's absolute misery for those out there without jobs, as well as for those whose jobs pay a pittance and offer no security. Unemployment will only get worse and so will the conditions in which they live. People are destitute.'

Noreen nods in agreement. 'When we were staying in our ancestral home in Ireland, Westport House, there were children outside the walls playing in the streets, even in the snow, without shoes while we lived wasteful, luxurious lives. And so it continues. I find it shocking. We spend as much as we want on things we don't even need while others get by with so very little. If I say this, people shrug their shoulders and turn away. It doesn't concern them.'

'Their sense of entitlement and their indifference appall me. I've made up my mind to walk away.'

'That's my plan too, if I can work out how to do it. The pointless luxury! The killing of blank hours and days! I'll go mad if I stay in that hothouse of boredom and selfishness.'

Noreen looks into the eyes of the serious, animated, handsome young man she has known for six hours and recognises a kindred spirit. A soulmate. As he does in her. She feels not a shred of doubt. They are cut from the same cloth. They understand exactly what they are rejecting and why. They see and worry about the gulf between their own privileged lives and those who have to get by in conditions that are barely fit for animals. They bring the same strong, clear intelligence to bear on the privilege and the inequality that are the bedrocks of their society. What fluke, what stroke of fate brought them to the same concert, to the same seats, in that audience of overblown aristocrats?

'I can't believe how we've managed to meet,' Noreen says, her eyes gleaming like a child at Christmas. 'If you hadn't gone to the concert, if you hadn't sat beside me...'

'Perhaps it wasn't luck,' Clive replies with an enigmatic smile.

'You went to find me?'

'Let's say your reputation goes before you. People gossip. I was interested to meet a young woman who is described as outspoken and unconventional. And rather difficult.'

'Who has been saying...'

'It doesn't matter.'

'You're right. It doesn't. But I thought you said you'd come to hear Fanny Davies.'

'Not exactly. If you remember, I asked you if you had heard her play because I already have.'

Noreen smiles. 'So you did.'

Clive reaches for Noreen's hand and covers it with his own. She lets it rest there.

'So what will you do?' she asks.

'As I said...I've enrolled at the Slade. I want to be a painter. I want to paint the working classes and the grim conditions in which they live and earn their wages. My intention is to move to a poor area so that I can observe things first hand, and paint scenes that are immediate and real. I mean to join groups and get involved in political action too. And you?'

'I've failed to be a concert pianist. It doesn't matter. It was never the right choice.'

Clive hears the chagrin behind the brave words, and understands that now is not the time to pursue it. 'Noreen, would you be willing to come with me? To work alongside me? We have energy and health and passion…there is so much we can do for those less fortunate than ourselves.'

'Of course,' she says with a simple conviction that will prove uncannily clairvoyant and correct. And long-lasting.

They continue meeting and ten days later decide to get married. It is May 1931.

When Clive and Noreen break the news to their respective families, which they do very quickly, there is outrage and opposition on both sides. Clive's parents are already reeling from the shock of their son's adamant intention to be a painter instead of a banker. Now, it seems, he is about to marry an actress called Noreen!

At a social gathering, they relay their misfortune to those willing, and eager, to hear.

'Is the surname Browne spelt with an e?' someone asks.

'Yes,' they reply. 'Her name is Noreen Browne.'

'Then she's not an actress. She's one of the richest heiresses in Europe, descended from Lord Sligo,' comes the reply.

How quickly one can change one's mind about a future daughter-in-law.

On the Browne side, things are not so easily resolved. There is disapproving talk about the Branson family earning their considerable fortune from business rather than from inheritance and bloodlines.

'You mustn't get involved with trade. It's vulgar!' Cicely remarks, mistakenly thinking that Noreen isn't serious.

'That's absurd,' Noreen replies. 'I don't care where Clive's money comes from, and I don't care if his father disinherits him! We will get married and live off what we earn.'

'You will wait, Noreen,' Cicely tells her, hoping that with the passage of time will come common sense.

'We don't want to wait. What's the point?'

'The convention is to be engaged for at least a year.'

'I don't care about convention.'

'But I do, and it is I who will organise your wedding and it is I who will have to face the pitying looks and disapproving comments of my family and friends if you get married to a man you have known for a few weeks, and later decide to leave because it was all a dreadful mistake. Do see reason, Noreen.'

'There is no mistake. I won't be leaving him, sooner or later. If you won't give your permission, I'll run away and live in sin.'

'You will do no such thing.'

'Oh, I will.'

And Cicely knows that Noreen is capable of just such an act of self-destruction. If she sets her mind to it, she won't think twice about flouting the wishes of her family – a family that stepped in when her parents died – and she'll risk being branded immoral. Her reputation will be in tatters. Living in sin…Cicely does a quick tally…is worse than marrying in a hurry. She decides she had better think of an excuse for the rushed marriage.

'So when are you and Clive hoping to marry?' Cicely asks, her face like thunder.

'In two weeks,' Noreen replies.

'It seems we must both compromise, and I do that against what I believe is right and proper. A girl needs to get to know a man and they, in turn, need to be introduced, as a couple, into the circles in which they will move…'

'We won't be moving in any circles. We'll be moving to Chelsea.'

'Chelsea?' Cecily shrieks, forgetting herself.

A black silence descends in which both women know they have reached an impasse.

\* \* \*

Noreen and Clive marry in June 1931 and move to a rented flat in the poorer part of Chelsea. They join the Independent Labour Party, and later the Communist Party, and commit to their shared, lifelong passion to help the poor and to fight for the rights of those who do not have a voice. Noreen works first as a researcher for Harry Pollitt, the General Secretary of the Communist Party, and then with the Labour Research Department, providing information and advice to more than fifty national trade unions, trades councils and other workers' organisations. Her first article for the LRD magazine appears in September 1938 and she continues to contribute to the magazine for sixty-five years.

Later she contributes £100,000 to fund the purchase of the building that will house the Marx Memorial Library in London.

Clive enrols at the Slade and paints with a dark energy and realism. He joins the Communist Party in his mid-twenties and forsakes painting for a while: 'He used to say that to be able to paint you must first learn about life.'[2] An active recruiter for the International Brigade, he goes himself to fight in the Spanish Civil War in January 1938 and is sent into action in March. In April, he is captured at Calaceite and sent to prison at San Pedro de Cardeña. In July he is transferred to an Italian concentration camp at Palencia where he paints the inmates at the request of the authorities. He is released on a prisoner exchange scheme. In an introduction to Clive Branson's British Soldier in India, Harry Pollitt writes: 'After the outbreak of the present war, while continuing his political work, he nevertheless spent a number of months painting very intensively, because, as he said, "it may be my last chance". He painted mainly the life in Battersea, where he lived, the workers in the streets, the events of the blitz.'[3] Six of his paintings hang in the Tate.

---

2. https://www.andrewwhitehead.net/blog/clive-branson-poet-artist-activist-soldier-writer
3. *British Soldier in India: the letters of Clive Branson.* Introduction by Harry Pollitt. Published London, *Communist Party, 1944.*

# 5 ON THE UPPER CLASSES

An extract from an interview
Rosa
2018

When Clive and Noreen married, my grandparents (Clive's parents) were horrified. My mother and father got married…and they had Christmas lunch with the family, and Granny was being bitchy about my father.

My mother lost her temper and said, 'Stop treating him like this!'

My father stood up and said, 'Noreen, let's leave this stupid thing and go home.'

And after that, Clive's mother treated him properly. Mummy was such a tough character, and anyway my grandparents were a bunch of snobs and my mother was Lady Noreen Browne, the daughter of a marquess. Well, you didn't argue with her! No, I think my grandmother realised that this daughter of a marquess was a very tough character.

Did she have siblings? Did they remain in their traditional roles?

Yes they did. My Aunt Sheelagh married John Treherne. He gambled all their money away. No, they followed the normal pattern.

Was your mother educated?

She wasn't allowed to go to university but she was allowed to study the piano.

Because then she could entertain future husbands.

Yes, she could entertain people in the drawing room. And one of my very early memories, when Daddy came home, was Mummy playing the piano and Daddy painting. The rest of them weren't particularly happy. Denis inherited

*Westport House. He was the one who came to me and said, 'God you're so lucky you don't have two miles of gutters.' They've sold it now. It was inherited by my cousin Jeremy who became the next marquess and when he died, his five daughters inherited it because he fixed it with the Irish government so that it could go to girls. They weren't particularly happy but they were immensely rich.*

*My cousin phoned me up about four years ago and said she felt her life had been a complete wreck. 'I think I've gone from riches to rags,' she said.*

'What do you mean?' I asked.

*'He's left me with four children.'*

*'Your idea of rags is a bit different from other people's,' I said.*

There must have been such wastage.

*There was! I know. I think it's still the same. But various people in Mummy's lot had been aristocrats and she didn't want anything to do with them.*

Did they know that their lives were empty?

*It was accepted.*

Very few seemed to leave the enclave.

*Well no, because it's so luxurious.*

But boring?

*So boring! They sat in these big stately homes.*

And entertained?

*Well, sometimes. Or they sat there reading and if they dropped the book on the floor, the footman would come in and pick it up for them. They hadn't seen people in rebellion. They didn't see anything else. You went to Ascot with the right people and you didn't meet the others. You didn't understand them and they didn't understand you. You didn't want to anyway. It's very simple.*

Has it changed?

*I don't think it has changed. The super rich are super rich and they're not happy. Of course they're not happy. They're always worried about their money. The very rich are scared of losing their money. And they're bored to death.*

*I was very lucky. My mother used to say, 'Provided you have enough to eat and you're warm and you have enough freedom to do what you think is important, you do not need tons and tons of money.'*

# 6 THE CHILD

# Her name is Rosa
# 1933

THEIR CHILD IS born in the week after the Reichstag fire, four weeks after Hitler was sworn in as Chancellor.

'Let's call her Rosa,' Noreen says, with a wicked look at Clive. The baby she holds in her arms is healthy, beautiful, wanted and adored.

'After Red Rosa Luxemburg,' Clive laughs. He is completely in love with his tiny daughter and committed to doing everything in his power to make her secure and happy. In years to come, on pages as yet unturned in Rosa's book of life, he will remain frozen as he is now. A young, adoring father.

They gaze at her wide-open eyes, stroke her peach soft fingers and touch her tiny nails of shell.

'But if Hitler invades England,' Clive says, his smile gone, 'then that name might be dangerous for her.'

'Heaven forbid. Is an invasion really likely, Clive?'

'Yes. The chances are high. There's a real risk.'

'And the name Rosa could condemn her? Truly?'

'I'm not going to be responsible for putting this baby in any kind of danger, no matter how hypothetical, no matter how unlikely, no matter how far in the future.'

'But she could be Rosa anything. Named after a rose. Who's going to make the link with Luxemburg?'

'With two parents known to be active in the Communist Party and perhaps already being monitored?'

'Really? Surely we're of no interest.'

'We're communists. All communists are of interest. Don't underestimate those who might make the link.'

'So we let others prevent us from calling our daughter by the name we choose?'

'We can't call her Rosa, Noreen.'

Clive registers his daughter as Mary Branson. This is the name on her birth certificate, her ration book and her identity card. But Noreen refuses to call her daughter anything but Rosa, and Clive, who loves and respects his wife, does the same.

It isn't until Rosa is twenty-one years old that she finds out that her name is Mary.


# Knees
## 1935
## Age 2 and a half

So many knees. Knees covered with the wavy hems of frocks, then stockings because the knees belong to women. For a long time in this new place, Rosa sees only knees unless she tips her head right back and looks up. Then the knees become bodies and the bodies have faces. There are children, but they are all bigger than she is. So it's either knees or a crick in the neck.

She had sat in the back seat of the car with a suitcase at her feet while Daddy drove and Mummy sat in the passenger seat. It was a long drive from Battersea, where they lived, to this big house in the country. Staring out of the window, Rosa had distracted herself by looking at the woods and fields, the cows and sheep, the hedgerows with rosebay and old man's beard, but she felt the atmosphere in the car, like the tight elastic of her knee-length socks. Mummy and Daddy were very quiet. They've told their daughter that she is starting school because Daddy will be going away soon to fight in a war in Spain. They've said it will be fun and she'll live with other children. Rosa didn't understand and hummed away the worry.

Now, under a tall tree whose copper leaves drift to the ground, a woman is bending down and taking hold of her hand. So bewildered is Rosa by the huge grounds and the children everywhere that for a moment she doesn't notice her parents slipping away. One minute they are at her side and the next they have gone.

'Rosa, isn't it?' the woman says in a kind voice, nodding to Clive and Noreen to leave.

'Where are Mummy and Daddy?' Rosa asks, looking around.

Dora holds Rosa's two hands in her own. 'They're going home. You're staying here with me. I'm Dora. This is my school and I hope you'll be very happy here. I'll be looking after you now. You should feel proud to be starting school because that's what big girls do.' The frown lines, which Rosa can't see, are at odds with the bright tone of her voice.

'I'm two and a half,' Rosa replies. 'I don't want to go to school. I want to go home.' She lifts her eyes from the knees, looks all the way down the long path that leads from the front door of the great house to a gate far away and sees two people walking away. They're small and getting smaller. Hard to see. Does one stop and turn round for a few seconds?

'Wait!' Rosa calls, pulling her hand from the woman's grip. 'Daddy! Wait for me!' She twists away and starts to run.

'No, Rosa,' Dora says, catching hold of the small girl and holding her by the shoulders. 'You aren't going home. Come on, let's go inside and I'll show you where you'll sleep and where you'll eat your meals and where you'll have your lessons, and you can meet some of the other children. Some are not much older than you.'

If Rosa had been able to look up into Dora Russell's face, she would have seen a cloud of anxiety passing over her composed features.

The youngest child I've ever taken, Dora Russell ponders with a sigh she can't hold in. Many years later, she will name Rosa as one of 'a lovable group of smalls' who made up the second intake after the school moved to Boyles Court in the autumn of 1934.[4] Now though, she feels the responsibility of a little girl who isn't yet three. I hope she'll settle, she thinks, as she walks the sad child inside.

Rosa can't pull her hand away. It's being held too hard. She wants to run after her mummy and daddy, but twisting her head, and looking again, she can't see them. Maybe they are getting in the car and driving away. Why are they leaving her here? The woman called Dora is leading her through heavy wooden doors and into a hallway full of echoes. Rosa doesn't remember the rest of that day.

She does remember feeling abandoned. In the pit of her stomach is a pain so big she doesn't know how she can bear it. The loss she feels is too vast for words. Too heavy for tears. The emptiness sits deep down inside her like an animal hunched and fearful, longing to escape but not knowing how. Rosa feels lost and trapped. A cage of sadness closes around her. She will remember this day for the rest of her long life. Later she will accept her mother's decision as rational and inevitable.

*I later asked my mother why she always got other people to care for me. It was understandable: she came from a family of aristocrats who traditionally never looked after their own children and had nannies, and she told me that in those days the experts said that the worst person to bring up a child was the mother.*

---

4. Russell, Dora. *The Tamarisk Tree, Vol 2: My School and the Years of the War.* Virago, 1981.

## First drawing
## 1937
## Age 4

Rosa is having her first drawing lesson at Dora Russell's school. The children are sitting at desks and they have a large piece of paper each and a pencil with a sharp tip. They are told to draw a house. Rosa thinks of her house where she lived before she came here. She thinks about it with Mummy and Daddy and herself together. She draws that house and she draws three people looking out of one of the windows. She draws their heads, bodies, arms and legs. Her teacher comes over and looks. And frowns.

'Rosa,' she says, 'if you can see people looking out of a window, you wouldn't be able to see their legs.'

*Rosa's first drawing of a house*

Rosa is upset at the unexpected criticism. She was eager and keen, and has tried her very best. It's her first drawing and she wanted so much to get it right.

## Communism and courtesy
## 1937 – 1939
## Age 4 and 5 and 6

Rosa is four and living at home with her mummy and daddy. She doesn't think of her hours and days as routine, but as her life as she knows it, as she likes it, as the life she missed when she was sent away to boarding school. The two years there were sad and slow and difficult. Now each day has its patterns and rhythms, its comings and goings, its times of starting and ending. For her, this house in Battersea is the best possible place to be. Love seeps through the rooms, the colour of red roses, the colour of strawberry jam, the colour her daddy calls crimson. She goes to a day school and comes home to sleep in her own bed. Gone are those hollow, hurting feelings of being alone and lonely and lost. The hard ache in her heart has melted away to leave a soft joy. She imagines pink blancmange, like her mummy makes, instead of the painful brown stones that lay heavily in the pit of her stomach. There is no-one walking away down a path, leaving her in a place that is not her home. They are three people under this roof. They are a family.

There is a question that won't go away and has attached itself inside her head like a fish hook. One day, with the fish-hook question hurting, she knows she has to say it out loud.

'Why did you send me away?' she asks.

Her mummy jumps up, pulls her daughter to her, wraps her arms around her and says, 'Only because it was the safest place for you. Your daddy and I were very busy and had to go away sometimes, so we decided the best place for you was at Dora Russell's school.'

'I didn't really like it,' Rosa says quietly.

'But you were looked after. And you were safe. It wasn't so bad, was it?"

Rosa can't make her mummy unhappy, so she decides it's all right to say nothing, which is like telling a little white lie, because it was bad. Her mummy hasn't really explained everything and the fish hook still sticks into a soft place.

'Did you go away because you wanted to help the Communist Party?' she asks.

'That's clever of you. Yes, I did.'

I know, Rosa thinks. That's where you and Daddy go to meetings in the evenings. I don't mind you leaving me because Granny is here to look after me, and you're always back when I wake up the next morning. Sometimes your communist friends come to the house and talk and talk round the kitchen table. What they say must be important because their voices grow loud and tumble over one another. Like waterfalls.

'When you were small, I went to India, to take some papers that were needed.' Noreen tells her daughter. What she doesn't tell her is that it was a highly dangerous mission but she doesn't need to elaborate.

'I know where India is. It's a very long way. How did you get there?'

'On a ship.'

Rosa considers this. Maybe her mother was crossing the ocean when she was at school.

'How long did it take?'

'Oh...a few weeks. I stayed a while, and then sailed back.'

'And then you were here?' Rosa asks, the fish-hook question niggling again.

'Only for a while. I went away again. A second time. To Europe, with more papers. I had to travel quite a bit, Rosa.'

Rosa breathes out. Her mother has given her a reason, a good reason, for sending her to school. They do love her.

The important thing, she tells herself, is that Mummy is here now, banging on the keys of her heavy typewriter or racing off to meetings, calling goodbye to her and Daddy, forgetting to change out of her raggedy cardigan. In the late afternoon, when the light fades to the blues and mauves of dusk, Mummy is always here. She lifts the lid of the piano and plays.

'A Chopin waltz,' she calls to her daughter.

'This is a Mozart sonata.'

'Do you like this one? It's called "Für Elise" by Beethoven.'

This is their unwinding time before dinner, when Daddy leaves his easel and stands behind Mummy, his paint-smeared hands on her shoulders. Noreen smiles up at him, her eyes shining.

One day, Rosa asks her fish-hook question again because it keeps snagging, not quite free. This time both her parents sit down with her in the evening and explain slowly and carefully why they had to send her to boarding school. Rosa remembers it clearly. They said her mummy might be sailing across oceans and her daddy was jailed in a Spanish prison and couldn't get home until they let him out. Goodness! We both escaped, Rosa thinks. She counts on her fingers. Her daddy was fighting or in prison for more than a year so of course he couldn't be at home for her. And her mummy kept going on ships for the Communist Party. It all makes sense now. She runs off to finish her drawing, while they carry on talking. They don't know that Rosa can listen very hard to grown-ups talking while pretending she is hard at work on a drawing. Like now. Mummy is asking Daddy to tell her the story of his time in prison again, and he thinks Rosa isn't listening. But she is. Oh! Rosa smiles to herself, as she too absorbs the story. They found out in the prison that he was connected in some important way to the Prince of Spain, and he told the prison commander they had better treat him a bit better. The commander sent one of his men to Madrid to buy Daddy some oil paints, but all the man could get were two blues and a yellow. Rosa shrugs her shoulders in delight.

Her mummy is roaring with laughter and asking, 'Darling, whatever did you paint?'

Daddy says, 'Six paintings of the other prisoners. The commander liked them so much he kept two, but I smuggled a few of the others back. They're somewhere around in one of the stacks over there.'

No wonder he doesn't know exactly where they are, Rosa thinks, because there are paintings everywhere.

*My daddy was a great big handsome funny bloke who did lovely paintings and he was such fun and made jokes. He came back from being imprisoned by Franco when I was four. I'd been sent to boarding school before then because my mother had gone as a spy to India, and then he came back and we were together for two years. We had lovely days out in the countryside, him painting and Mummy reading, it was such fun.*

Rosa is allowed to stand at her father's side and watch him paint, in fact Clive thinks it normal and natural for her to be there. This is part of her education. She knows how to be still and silent. A long time later, when Rosa is studying art at Camberwell College, she rejects her tutors' instructions to paint the *'dustbins and Camberwell in the rain'* in fashionable daubs, but this is what her daddy is painting – the faces of the people who live in the slums not far away and who, he tells her, work in unsafe, unhealthy places. He wants to paint their lives in all their sad detail.

'To be able to paint, you must first learn about life,' he tells his daughter.

Rosa watches the faces take shape on his canvases, the strong browns and blacks and the deep shadows showing their exhaustion and despair. He's a wonderful artist, Rosa thinks. These faces are so real I could reach up and touch them and feel each person's skin. I want to be a painter when I grow up, like Daddy. I want to be as good as he is.

There are framed canvases and paintings stacked against walls. On tables and shelves are jars of brushes and paints. There's not much space to move around but no-one minds. After long hours at his easel, Clive shrugs off his smock and chases his little daughter from room to room and when he catches her, he throws her in the air, making her shriek with laughter.

One day, Rosa is drawing on the kitchen table when her parents come to her with solemn faces. Oh no. For a moment she waits to hear that their life is about to change again. Which one of them is going away? They both bob down, level with her, and talk to her quietly and with great respect.

'Darling, would you mind very much if we take down some of your drawings on the wall in the hall and over the stairs because, you see, there's no space to hang Daddy's paintings?'

'Sorry, Rosa,' Clive adds, pulling a rueful face, his hands clasping both of hers. 'I'm sorry to ask you to move your drawings. They're very good. Only I'm running out of floor space and tripping over the frames. And I need to look at my paintings on a wall, level with my eyes, so I can see what works and what doesn't work. Do you understand?'

Of course she understands! Rosa is surprised and amazed. Why are these two adults asking her permission? She is a child of four and her daddy is a proper artist. Of course his paintings must hang on the walls.

'Do you understand?' her mother asks again. 'Do you mind terribly?'

'Of course I understand,' Rosa replies. 'And I don't mind at all.'

Rosa is up and running to the hall where she stands beneath a drawing she's done of her mummy and daddy. She hops from one foot to the other, impatient for them to unpin it and hand it down to her.

'No hurry, Rosa,' her father calls. 'Tomorrow will do fine. Thank you, darling.'

*They felt it mattered what I did. I realised that they took me seriously and I would always try to do my best to live up to their aspirations.*

In bed that night, Rosa plays the scene again, her parents crouched down, faces composed, asking her if she minds if they take down her drawings. She doesn't yet have the words to phrase this as she will when she is older, but she hears their concern, their decency and politeness. Is this what being a communist means? When she grows up, she will be like them.

Another day, another late afternoon with a father at his easel, a mother at the piano and a child at the kitchen table with a paint box. Rosa is absorbed in creating the delicate filigree wings of fairies in palest pink and blue. Her bedtime story drops her nightly into the magical world of these little creatures who, like her parents, do good and help people with miniature acts of kindness. She dips her brush in the jar and waters down her blocks of colour to create tiny figures who are almost transparent, almost not there, almost invisible. The flowers they live in can be brighter. So deep in concentration is she that she is unaware of her mother rising from the piano to put the kettle on and of her father wandering across and looking down over her head.

'Noreen, why is our daughter painting fairies?' Clive asks with convincing solemnity.

Bringing two mugs to the table, Noreen stands at his side and looks at her daughter's work. 'What's wrong with fairies?' she asks. 'And she's painting them beautifully. Look at the detail on the wings.'

'Surely as two committed communists, we should be teaching her how to paint the working classes,' he replies, a hand round her waist.

Rosa puts down her brush, looks up and catches the glint of amusement that passes between them.

'Nonsense. If she wants to paint fairies, she should be allowed to paint fairies,' her mother replies. 'No-one tells you what to paint.'

Rosa remembers feeling proud and honoured that her parents are discussing her paintings with such seriousness. What she paints clearly matters to them. It's another moment in her young life that is caught, held and treasured. She recalls it decades later as clearly as an image caught with a camera. Does Rosa not also feel, on her four-year-old shoulders, the responsibility of living up to those standards and ideals? Is there not a burden there? When I venture the question, she says, *Absolutely not.*

## Smashing gas lamps
## 1939
## Age 6

*'For two years until the start of the war... I had such a happy time.'*

There is a new busyness and movement in the house with her mummy pulling pans and crockery out of cupboards and packing them with crumpled newspaper in boxes. She puts most of their clothes, and there aren't many, into old suitcases. There seems to be no urgency because her daddy carries on painting and her mummy still plays the piano in the evenings so Rosa doesn't take much notice. Perhaps they're having a tidy-up to make more room because they are very crammed in the small rooms and they're always tripping over things. Especially paintings and easels.

'We're moving to 4, Glycena Road, Rosa. Lavender Hill. In Battersea,' Noreen tells her daughter one day and Rosa's heart skips with excitement. Maybe it will be lovely. She practises saying her new address out loud until she knows it by heart. Then if she ever gets lost, she can ask someone to help her find her way home.

Perhaps she is remembering her Branson grandparents' big, imposing house hidden from the road and set in splendid grounds, but Rosa is distinctly unimpressed with Glycena Road. They pull up outside a tall gloomy house, one of many in long terraces on both sides of the road with steps straight down to the pavement and no front garden. They stand beside the car and wait for the van with their things, and in those first waiting moments, Rosa stares up at the ugly house in astonishment. Why would any grown-up choose to live here? Why have her parents picked such a horrible place? The houses loom up, almost blocking out the light. The street feels dark and cold. Rosa doesn't want to hurt her parents' feelings by saying what she feels so she looks up at the strip of sky above the buildings, her face set in a frown. The sky's the only beautiful thing in sight. Standing on the pavement, she feels oppressed by these houses and worries that she will be starved of sunlight. She will droop, like flowers planted in too much shade.

They have the top half of the house where the sun does come in the windows for a few hours every day, slanting over roofs before it vanishes again below the houses opposite. It must be horribly gloomy in the bottom half where Mr and Mrs Sutters and their daughter live.

For a week there's a lot of bustling and unpacking and sorting out until the place begins to feel like home and everyone settles into their familiar routine again. Her father sets up his easel and is soon at work. Rosa watches him painting the streets where they now live and the men in caps and women in aprons who work in the factories. So he doesn't find it ugly, she thinks, or at least he finds it interesting enough to paint. His paintings are not pretty, but they're very good. She hears people who come to the house say how good they are and she agrees. Staring out of them are worn-down, tired people with lines on their foreheads and soot on their faces. They seem angry or defeated, and shout silently at her in hoarse voices. There are pavements and yards with people doing dirty, heavy work. Her mother bangs away on her typewriter. Her parents seem happy and don't once complain about the house being dark, the street ugly, the neighbourhood rough and very poor. They rush out to meetings held in a hall nearby and come back excited and full of plans. People come to this new house, like they did to the old one, and sit up half the night talking in loud voices. Noreen notices her daughter is still up, sitting very still in a corner, and takes her up to bed, but not before Rosa has heard enough big words and long sentences to give her a glimpse into their grown-up world. Fair pay. Decent conditions. Workers' rights. Capitalism. Communism. A man called Marx.

Despite the important gatherings, Mummy finds time to complain that the milk doesn't have any cream on the top. One day she tells the milkman who says, 'Well, when I deliver it, it has cream on the top.' Mummy has her suspicions and stands like a spy at the window in her dressing gown very early in the morning, waiting to catch the culprit. And she does. She sees Mrs Sutters sneaking out from downstairs as soon as the milkman has placed her bottles and ours side by side on the step. Mrs Sutters takes all the bottles inside, then quickly reappears carrying just our bottles. She is acting oddly, shutting her door without making a sound, looking around, glancing quickly up at the top windows. Very suspicious, Rosa thinks. The tops on our bottles are always a bit crinkled and now Mummy knows why. She tells Rosa she will confront Mrs Sutters the following morning.

Just as the neighbour is putting our bottles back on the step, Mummy storms downstairs and flings open the door.

'You've been taking the cream off our milk and filling the bottles up with water, haven't you?' Mummy says. 'Don't you dare do it again.'

'I've done no such thing,' Mrs Sutters replies, going inside and slamming her door.

But it doesn't happen again. The milk on my porridge is creamy and rich. I am proud of my mummy for shouting at Mrs Sutters.

Each evening, the children who live in Glycena Road tumble outside onto the street, energy fizzing, like wild animals freed from cages.

'Vagabonds and gypsies,' Noreen remarks approvingly. 'Yes, you can go and play with them, Rosa.' Then she resumes her typing.

So Rosa does. And notices the rips and tears in the children's thin clothes and the holes in their shoes. She sees that in winter they have icy white hands and their faces look pinched. Their legs are bare, their knees scraped and their old saggy socks tumble in folds around their ankles. The boys look like they've never been washed and wear great big caps set at a jaunty angle on their heads. They've found a cricket bat from somewhere and they bowl and bat for hours down the middle of the street, once sending a ball through someone's window. Then they run for dear life and Rosa runs screaming after them.

There's a gang of older boys who don't play games in the street. They roam round the neighbourhood, shouting and kicking things along the gutters, pinching stuff. The grown-ups call them vandals. They're always in trouble and they couldn't care less. Rosa watches them with awe when they sweep past, sometimes teasing and taunting the younger ones, giving anyone who gives them cheek a slap around the ears. But no-one bothers Rosa, not after one of the lads starts to hang about near her and watches out for her, like he's decided to keep her under his wing. They chat. They laugh. He slaps her on the back. Maybe he understands her tough spirit because soon she's tagging along at his side, a small girl trying to keep up with a strong twelve-year-old boy, running as fast as she can in the wind and the rain, a ragamuffin of a child, her hair wild over her shoulders and her cardigan sliding off her shoulders. His name is Leo and the other children are wary of him, scared of his quick temper, frightened that he'll turn on them with his fists. Rosa is drawn to him, tells him she likes and trusts him, and senses him protecting her in their child's world that is rough and tough and brutal, and where tempers flare quickly and stomachs are achingly empty. There'll be no favours for her because she's a girl and only six, but Leo seems to sense a kindred spirit. And Rosa may be the only person in his difficult life who has told him that she trusts him.

When night starts to fall, Rosa and Leo and the other boys in the gang race to neighbouring streets and hurl rocks and stones at the gas lamps. They howl with laughter and throw their arms in the air in victory when they hit one square on and it goes dark. Shattered glass falls at their feet and they tread and jump on it, crunching it to tiny sparkly bits. Rosa has a good aim for someone so young. Leo claps her on the back when she too hits one of the lamps and she glows with pleasure. On bonanza evenings they put out several lights and the streets turn dark. After hours of lovely naughty violence, Leo holds Rosa's hand and walks her back to her house through the now dark streets. She is triumphant. He deposits her on the steps, nods to her, and runs off in search of more mischief. Rosa goes inside, glad that she lives on Glycena Road. Noreen is waiting with a smile and a hug.

Rosa is now running around regularly with the gang of older boys and looks feral like them. One day, a neighbour stops Noreen as she's fishing for her key to open her front door, and asks to have a word. It's obvious she's been waiting to pounce. Her lips are sour-looking and she tuts under her breath. Does Mrs Branson know, the woman asks, that her daughter is mixing with a bad lot and will get into trouble? Noreen pauses only for a moment, glances at Rosa at her side, then inserts the key and goes inside. The woman gets no reply, but Noreen shakes her head with disapproval. With her, Rosa wonders? Days later, another neighbour, who lives a few houses away, corners Noreen when she's buying food from the shop at the end of the road. The woman stares at Rosa with disapproval, puts a hand on Noreen's sleeve and asks her, with quiet self-importance, if she is aware that her daughter is running around the streets with a gang of boys.

'They're a bad lot, especially that Leo,' the woman says. 'You need to keep a closer eye on your daughter.' The woman expects to be thanked.

For a moment Rosa holds her breath, worried that her fun is about to end. But her mother stares back at the woman and says, 'I know and I don't see any harm in him. He isn't a capitalist, therefore he is all right.' They leave the woman standing there with her mouth open. Rosa looks up at her mother with admiration.


## The tiger with the flaming eyes
## 1939
## Age 6

The tiger in the rhododendron bushes has fiery flames flashing from his eyes and stares at Rosa from behind the glossy leaves. She stares back, not one bit frightened. She's thrilled that he has shown himself to her and stoops to part the leaves so that she can admire the flickering fire, his fine yellow and brown stripes, his swinging tail. It's break time at Beltane School where Rosa attends as a day pupil. The other children are racing around or playing catch, and as usual Rosa has wandered off on her own after being firmly rejected.

'Go away!' they always shout when she goes anywhere near their games.

'You're hopeless at games.'

'We don't want you!'

'Can't catch a ball!'

Yes, she's useless at throwing and catching balls. She can't even see the ball, let alone grab hold of it when it hurtles towards her. Sometimes it hits her smack in the stomach or shoulder. A few times painfully in her face. So she sidesteps, or like now, simply doesn't join in. Later, her grandmother will find out that Rosa is long-sighted and needs glasses, but for now she appears simply useless at all games and not worth bothering with.

The bell goes and the children wander back inside, but Rosa waits beside the tiger, entranced and enamoured. She rushes in last. Late. 'There's a tiger with flaming eyes in the bushes,' she shouts to the settling class. 'Quick! Come and see!'

While some children decide it's safer to stay inside, others race after Rosa screaming and shouting. The boys pick up sticks and wave them as weapons, ready to bravely attack. Or defend. The teacher is so taken by surprise by this strange child's behaviour that she is unable to put a stop to the mass exodus, and it will be a while before she can restore control and funnel the children back to their desks.

'There!' Rosa says triumphantly, pointing to the still-crouching animal with the fantastic eyes.

'Cant see it!' the other children shout.

'Of course you can,' she counters. 'There!'

Some of the boys pretend they can and swipe at the bushes with their sticks, breaking stems and scattering broken flower heads and bruised leaves.

'You don't have to attack the tiger!' Rosa tells them, shocked. 'Just look at it. It's beautiful.' But her advice falls on deaf ears.

When order is finally restored and the children are back in their seats, the teacher summons Rosa to the front of the class.

'That was a very silly thing to do. You are not to play that trick again, Rosa.'

'It wasn't a trick.'

'There was no tiger in the bush.'

'There was.'

'Rosa, we are in England. Tigers live in India.'

'I could see a tiger.'

'Then you need your eyes testing. It was a trick to get some attention. Now go back to your seat and get on with your work.'

Yes, Rosa does need her eyes testing, but not because she sees a tiger in the flowerbed. She struggles to see anything close up. However much she squints at her reading book, and at the chalk squiggles on the blackboard, letters appear as a blur of grey and words run together as swirly as water. Yet it will be three more years before the glaringly obvious connection is made between Rosa's poor eyesight and her inability to learn to read. *Finally my grandparents discovered that I needed glasses. I was long-sighted which was why I didn't learn to read until I was nine.* Until then, the black and white of letters on blackboards and words on paper will swim together, opaque and completely unreadable, while the visions will be precise and exact. And so very welcome.

The visions continue throughout Rosa's life. *In Battersea, I would wake every morning to see an old woman sitting at a table opposite my bed, but when I got up she turned into my mother's typewriter.* She accepts them, and uses them in her paintings. Experienced by many other artists, she describes them as a gift, but also as a very normal, ordinary part of her days. *I use them all the time. When you have a day off, you go round looking at things because you're not painting and you're seeing things all the time...I can imagine a dragon coming from behind the stalls or a person behind the desk with horns. It could be anywhere. Sometimes they're sunlight, sometimes they're shimmering water, sometimes they're birds...you just don't know. It's a very awake state but if you think it's real, you have mental problems. It's an image. It's not real.*

## Polperro and Melksham
## 1939 – 1940
## Age 6 and 7

During her weeks boarding at Beltane School, and on the weekends back at home, Rosa catches snippets of adult conversations as people everywhere talk about something called 'the Phoney War'. Noises off, someone says. Rumours, says another. Fear is put tentatively on hold. For eight months, from September 1939 to April 1940, Hitler stands ready, but does not invade. It's a brief lull and a short false dawn. Her mother tells her that war has been declared by Neville Chamberlain but not to worry because nothing seems to be happening. Not yet.

While war is in a limbo place, Rosa is at relative peace. When a longing to live at home all the time threatens to overwhelm her and brings floods of tears, she reminds herself sternly that her mummy has enrolled as an air raid warden, doing her duty, so it's selfish and silly of her to feel sorry for herself. Rosa, she tells herself, you are lucky, but she doesn't feel it.

And then something wonderful happens. Rosa's class, the youngest pupils at Beltane School, is evacuated to Polperro in Cornwall, to the safety and comfort of a lovely old house on the edge of the pier where they are cared for with kindness by the mother of Mrs Tomlinson, one of the school's owners. The house is warm and comfortable. The food is good and plentiful. It could almost be that England has forgotten about war.

During this interlude of calm, when the world waits for war, Rosa wakes to the sound of waves splashing against the wooden planks of Polperro pier. She hears the cry of gulls circling low over the fleet of small fishing boats that are made ready for the day's catch with nets loaded on deck by men with wind-reddened faces. With the sun streaming in the window, there is every reason for Rosa to jump out of bed, eager to start her day. If sadness accompanies her on her way downstairs, she pushes it away. There are blessings here.

The sea is her close companion, a constant presence, rolling its way up and down the long sandy beach with a soothing predictability, sloshing up to the slippery seaweed line then rippling back over the rattling pebbles, dislodging many as it goes. Each day is the same. Rosa tastes salt in the air and scratches at the grains of sand that sneakily work their way under her clothing no matter how carefully she pulls up her stockings and buttons up her coat. After lessons, her hat is off and she runs free. Picking up a long, slimy skein of seaweed, she runs fingers over the dark shine of its surface and pops the little bubbles down the centre of its curvy length. She is quite good at drawing now. But can she paint its exact colour which is neither quite black nor quite brown? Can she capture the glossy sheen? Her every footstep crunches on shells of every size and colour. Head down, she picks out the perfect ones, the pearly ones, the ones that have not been hurt, the ones she will keep in her box. How to reproduce their light-filled swirls with her paints? She remembers her daddy showing her how to make white out of red, green and blue. Titanium White is too bright and blue-toned and doesn't have the precious pink tones of the shells.

On fine days, she is allowed to peel off her annoyingly thick stockings, leave them in a careless pile with her shoes and cardigan, and squelch barefoot along the frothing, foaming edge of the sea. With the other children, and with her teacher keeping a watchful eye, she ventures in, again and again, as far as she dares, playing a game with the sneaky waves that all of a sudden come rushing in with an unexpected surge, soaking the hem of her frock. Once wet, she might as well splash until her feet are too icy cold to feel the stones and shells on the seabed. How do I paint the water, she wonders, with the sunshine breaking its surface into dazzling pinpoints of light. How do I paint waves that never stay still but overlap and expand and make transparent windows of stillness before their pattern rolls on again? Her daddy once told her that the sea is blue, not transparent, because water absorbs colours in the red part of the light spectrum, like a filter, leaving behind only the blues, but he didn't paint the sea. He painted the houses and factories in Battersea and the people who lived and worked in them. Browns and reds, not turquoise and blue.

Cold now, and still thinking about the colours of the sea, she high-steps out of the waves. Back on the sand, it's impossible to pull stockings over sticky, sand-coated feet and legs. Sometimes she runs back barefoot, holding the offending articles of clothing. No adult will reprimand her. Mrs Tomlinson's mother runs this temporary wartime shelter with a gentle kindness.

During this breath-held lull, war waits in the wings.

One day, Rosa comes down to breakfast in the house by the pier to find Mrs Tomlinson looking grave.

'I have some rather bad news for you,' she tells the children. 'Our country has declared war with Germany. It's not safe for you to live here on the coast anymore because this is where the enemy planes will fly across from Germany and enter our skies to drop their bombs.'

Her announcement is greeted with gasps, although for these young children the meaning of war is still unsubstantial. The word, heard often on the lips of adults, carries only a vague fear.

'Let me explain. Beltane School is evacuating all its pupils to a great big house in the country, near Bath. That's where you're going too, so today is your last day here. You'll be living in grand style and be very comfortable. I'm sad that you're going. I've enjoyed looking after you. Later, we will pack up and get you all ready to go.'

Sighs circulate the kitchen table combined with a crackle of expectation and excitement. Another move. Another place to live. Rosa is unimpressed.

'I like it here,' she says, so quietly that no-one hears.

The scaling down of her life from a large noisy boarding school to a house by the sea has suited her because she feels more comfortable in a small group and in a quieter, more domestic context. The backdrop of an ever-changing yet constant sea and sky soothes her. She has not been unhappy here. Before she leaves, she takes out her sketchpad and, looking out of her bedroom window, draws the seagulls swooping in arcs in a dance of flight. The finished sketch satisfies her.

The following morning, cars line the pavement ready to take the children and their suitcases on a long, tedious journey. It will try even the most patient of them. Later, as the sun drops down the sky, they are far too tired to take in the great, stately house in Melksham with its acres of rolling lawns and gardens and rooms too numerous to count. For now, this place just has a label: our next school; our next home. The older children are already here and, the young ones are told, have begun to settle in.

Is it weeks or months later? Rosa can't remember. A rare and unexpected visit from her mother brings the news that she is to move school yet again.

'So soon?' Rosa asks. 'Are we not safe from the bombs here?'

'No, it's not that. You're perfectly safe here.'

'Then why?'

'Darling, I'm sorry to disrupt you again, but Bath is too far away from London and I can't get here to see you as often as I would like. You see, because I'm working as an air raid warden, I only get a few hours off and that's not long enough to make the journey here and back. I miss you. Daddy is away fighting and you are all I have.'

Rosa hears the slight tremble in her mother's voice and understands that she is being moved for a very good reason. She accepts the decision without complaint. Wherever it is she is going, she will see her mother more often, and that is more important than anything else.

When Noreen has gone, Rosa wanders round the stately home and its grounds, saying goodbye to a place she barely knows and where she has no roots. The front lawn is vast, perfectly mowed and rolled, and serves as the county cricket pitch with men in white carrying bats arriving to play on Saturdays. Loud shouts and the thwack of wood on ball echo all round the house and the children have to keep a safe distance. Empty now, Rosa crosses its great length and lingers in the enclosed rose gardens, dropping her head into the heady scent, then holding one perfect scroll of petals under her nose. Which colour does she like best? The deepest, darkest reds or the fragile whites or the less exact apricots and yellows? She would paint them in the large art room, but she won't be here much longer. There are no roses in her daddy's paintings. Remembering him laughing at her painting fairies, she wonders if he would approve of her painting flowers. 'The working classes don't have gardens,' he might tell her. 'Or if they do, they are put to good use for vegetables so the people don't starve. Flowers are a luxury. Only the wealthy pick great scented bunches of roses and arrange them in cut glass vases. I want my daughter painting potatoes and cabbages, not roses,' is something else he might tell her, with a big grin.

# Hollyhocks
## 1940
## Age 7

Rosa is weary to her bones of being picked on and teased and bullied because of something that she didn't do. Her skin feels scraped clean to leave only raw nerve endings. Alone, and where no-one can see her, she sobs in the empty kitchen and sheds tears in dark hidden corners of the sprawling gardens. In front of others, she tries her very best to be strong and brave because the worst thing of all would be to make Mummy or Daddy ashamed of her. But it's been a whole year and she's quite worn down. She thinks back, as she often does, to the cruel untrue accusation and sighs deeply at the unfairness of it all. Mummy and Daddy are never unfair. They believe in fairness for everyone. They believe in the truth. They are communists.

This is what happened. She had wandered out of the great building into the gardens during a break in lessons, alone as she often was because she doesn't make friends easily. She senses that she is different and not like other seven-year-olds, and so she is often lonely. For one thing, her eyes trouble her, not that she questions her poor sight because she has known nothing different. She knows that anything held close up is blurred, just as figures in the distance start out clear and turn vague and swirly as they approach her. She has to squint at children and teachers who stand at her side. Distant lawns and sky are sharp shapes of green and blue, and animals grazing in far fields have solid outlines. Words on a page are a mystery. It will be two more years before her grandmother discovers that Rosa needs glasses. Astonishingly, up to now, not a single teacher has thought to ask if perhaps Rosa has problems with her sight. The general consensus is that she's not very bright. A difficult, unpopular child, they say amongst themselves. They lose patience and can be unkind. Rosa sighs deeply at her predicament. Mummy and Daddy treat her with respect. They don't tell her she's stupid.

On the rough steps, something glitters in the sun, catching her attention and pulling her away from her yearning to be home. She can't see what it is, but bends to pick it up, turns it over in her hand and strokes its cool surface. Touch immediately tells her it's a key, but for which door? For a while she carries it around the gardens, thinking of doors opening, after being unlocked, to reveal secrets. She imagines a key that opens a door to a room where her mummy is typing and her daddy is painting. They smile and call her to them. Of course none of this is true because her country is about to go to war and Mummy has signed up to do dangerous work as an air raid warden and her daddy may already have gone to fight. Tuning into her mother's mood, as she often does, Rosa knows she will be unhappy if Clive is not with her. Rosa is telepathic and picks up her mother's emotions, however far apart they might be. Knowing her mother is depressed is a worry and she carries that grown-up sadness as an extra weight on her small shoulders. Rosa turns her attention back to the key, liking its metallic coldness, and for a long time is lost to her imaginings. When the bell rings for lessons, she puts it in her pocket and forgets about it.

It's not until supper that she puts her hand in her pocket and feels the cold object hiding in the fabric folds. Oh, she should have handed it in sooner. She puts down her fork, stands up to speak, holding out the key in her hand. Matron, who misses nothing, is at her side in seconds. Rosa no longer remembers the exact words but the tall woman is extremely angry.

'That's the key to the storeroom,' she says. 'You know where that is, and you know what's inside. There's a war on and we're rationed. You were trying to steal more than your fair share of food, weren't you?'

'I found the key on the step,' Rosa replies.

'You're a liar, Rosa Branson. A wicked liar.'

All the children have stopped eating. Silence hangs around her like a curtain. They are listening to every word that's said.

'I didn't steal it,' Rosa speaks up. 'I found it on the step.'

'No-one would have left that key on a step. You're lying.'

'I did find it on the step. Outside.'

'I don't believe you. You're a liar. You will be punished.'

The punishment Rosa receives from Matron is nothing compared with the punishment which almost every child in the school metes out over the next year. As if they've been waiting for this chance to torment her. They have always sensed that she is different from them, and now they have something definite on which to hang their suspicion and mistrust. They taunt. They tease. They shout. They accuse. They refuse to play with her. They push her and trip her up. They call her, 'Liar! Liar!'

For Mummy's sake and for Daddy's, Rosa has tried her best to put up with it and has told no-one, but today she can't take any more. Someone told her that hollyhocks are poisonous so she can put an end to her troubled life by eating their flowers. She heads for the herbaceous borders where they grow with other plants in splendid profusion, their pinks mixing with white, cream, yellow and red. No-one can see her as she bends into the bushes, pulls off the flower heads and crams them into her mouth. They taste of perfume and grass. She eats and eats, pink juice seeping from her lips, as much as she can stomach, before running back inside. Now she will die. She sees it as a solution to all her sorrows. An ending.

Rosa resumes her place, quiet and composed, waiting to die. She is glad the other children will finally understand how sad she is and how much they've upset her. In death they might be kind to her. There will be a small coffin with pretty flowers on top. She waits. The lesson continues. It's taking a long time for the poison to work and a ghastly thought crosses her mind. Is it possible that some hollyhocks aren't poisonous? Then another ghastly thought. Should she have eaten an awful lot more for them to kill her? Because nothing is happening. Not even a stomach ache.

'Rosa, why aren't you writing?' A voice breaks into her thoughts.

Rosa sighs deeply and picks up her pencil. She must endure.

*I was so miserable. I was very lonely. The trouble with the evacuation business was that all the kids were miserable and therefore the tough ones bullied the others and I was the sort who was always in floods of tears. I was bullied all the time. I was the little one who couldn't fight back and it wasn't until I learnt how to use art to fight back* (by drawing caricatures of people who were unpleasant, unkind and stupid) *that I felt that I was in control. Before that I didn't know how to cope with it. I just felt so lonely.*


## Newsreel at the station
## Paddington
## 1944
## Age 10

Rosa has been moved to Springfield Grange School, a farm school in Great Missenden, Buckinghamshire, chosen by Noreen for her daughter's own protection. It's a place of security away from the deathly destruction that is the Blitz.

Her short break from boarding school is over, made briefer than usual by Noreen's determination to keep her daughter well away from the falling bombs and heartbreaking wreckage that is war. In Battersea, the Blitz is everyday life. Noreen's work is more dangerous than ever.

It's been a quiet, subdued break. Some evenings, Rosa watches Noreen jam on her helmet to go out to patrol the streets and she worries. Although Noreen tells her daughter very little, Rosa knows it's dangerous work and she waits with a hard-beating heart until her mother is safely home again. If she goes to bed, she lies awake waiting for the sound of the key in the lock.

Rosa is sometimes alone in the house, worrying and drawing. Knowing there's a war on, she colours everything a shade darker, as if the sun is always behind a cloud and everyone lives in shadow. Daddy is fighting in Burma. She and Noreen don't talk about it because it's too difficult and too upsetting, but they both carry an image of Clive in a trench or under fire, wherever they go and whatever they do.

'We have to be brave, Rosa. We must carry on. There are people having a much harder time than us.'

'I know, Mummy, but I can't forget about Daddy fighting.'

'I'm not saying forget, darling. Just keep that knowledge to yourself and keep believing that he will come home safely.'

'It's hard.'

Noreen sighs. Yes, it's very hard. 'I know. I find it hard too so I keep busy with my writing and my war work.'

'You're brave, Mummy. You don't show that you're worried.'

'I do what I have to do. We all must.'

But Rosa senses her mother's silent but gnawing anxiety and walks with deadening weights on her young shoulders.

They wait for letters from Burma, each one a confirmation that Clive is still alive, at least at the moment of writing from his tent or from a muddy trench where he lies in hiding. Inside every letter, he encloses a stamp on which he has written a tiny letter in tiny words for Rosa. These mean so very much. Her beloved daddy makes time, while living in some horrible place, fighting a dangerous enemy, to send her small messages of love, penned in miniature letters on little squares of paper he has saved specially for her. After reading them many times – because now she can read even the smallest print – she puts them in a safe place and keeps them. All her long life, she keeps those letters written on stamps.

Rosa's small leather case is ready-packed. She's only taking clean clothes and handkerchiefs, and some books and new pencils Mummy gave her.

'It's time to go,' Noreen says, appearing in the hall and looking distracted, as she often does. She grabs a jacket from the hall cupboard and pushes her arms into it. At ten, Rosa is old enough to notice that her mother's jacket is ragged round the hem and she's forgotten her hat. Noreen shrugs on the first thing to hand, always in a hurry, and she doesn't stop to look in the mirror. The other day she went out in a cardigan with a huge hole in the sleeve. It pleases Rosa that her mother looks like a gypsy with wild hair and ladders in her stockings and no lipstick.

'What does it matter?' Noreen says, when Rosa points to a big hole. 'Who cares what I look like?'

'Well, Granny certainly does.' Rosa replies with a smirk. 'The other day she said you insist on wearing dreadful shabby old clothes and have no style.'

'Style!' Noreen snorts. 'There's a war on.'

It's the stock answer to almost everything.

Noreen drives them to Paddington and parks the car in a side street. People are coming and going with bags and suitcases, the station a bustling place of movement and noise. Long before she reaches the entrance, Rosa can hear the engines puffing and whistling steam and men shouting orders.

Paddington is more like a cathedral than a station, she thinks, its great iron arches forming a latticework tunnel burnished only in squares and shafts by the sky above. Rosa has to lean back to see the intricate criss-crossing metal and asks herself, always, how she could possibly draw such a mighty construction. The engines snort plumes of sooty smoke while they wait, like dragons, soon to be fired up for their next journey. When the stokers pile on the coal, they roar and vibrate, the pistons creaking round slowly at first, then harder and faster until the engine nudges forwards, dragging the carriages out of the station. Standing next to one of these monstrous engines, Rosa always feels very small, a bit dizzy and a bit afraid.

Usually they walk straight to the platform, Rosa boards her train, finds a seat by the window and waves a quick goodbye to her mother who, after waving back, turns and walks away. It doesn't do to make a fuss. Today, Noreen hesitates, then stops at the entrance to the small cinema in the station where Pathé newsreels are running all day and all night showing recent footage of the war. Passengers who have the time, and workers on lunch breaks, linger and watch, drawn to the horror. There's quite a crowd. All the seats are taken. Noreen and Rosa stand at the back because the train will depart in about fifteen minutes. Rosa is only just able to see the screen between the heads and shoulders huddled in front of her. They hear the newsreader's crisp voice: '…in this forbidding land of Burma…' Noreen stands stock-still. Why has she walked in today, of all days, to watch the news? Premonition? A whisper in her ear? A cry from a soldier she loves who is fighting in a land far away? Rosa absolutely believes in such things because she, like Noreen, is clairvoyant. Both see the future.

On the screen soldiers in tin helmets stuck with twigs and carrying rifles are stumbling through dense woodland, crawling on their bellies, running with stretchers carrying wounded comrades. There's smoke and fire and dust. It's real and horrible and terribly dangerous. The Japs have laid booby traps that explode in blasts of fire that hurt and maim and kill. Rosa holds her breath. Noreen is rigid at her side. The camera moves to a close-up of a soldier who has fallen, his body held and covered by the undergrowth. Only his shoulders and arms are visible. His helmet has been knocked forwards so his face is hidden. Other soldiers race to his side but there's nothing they can do for him. He's dead. The newsreader articulates precisely, 'There is heavy fighting on the Arakan Pass.' Mummy gasps. One hand flies up to her mouth. Her other hand tightens around her daughter's so hard it hurts. Worried, Rosa glances up. Her mummy's face is as white as chalk. Like a ghost. Like a clown without the red nose. If she painted her mummy's face now, she would use her tube of Titanium White and not add any flesh tints. The two of them are squashed close enough for Rosa to feel her mother shaking. She looks back at the screen. She hears the sound of gunfire. She watches soldiers who are not dead running up a steep hill, their rifles held ready to fire. More stumble and fall.

'What's the matter?' Rosa asks, very quietly so as not to disturb the others watching. Noreen doesn't reply. She spins round and pulls her daughter out of the cinema, her lips white, her eyes glinting, maybe with tears. She walks very quickly, leading Rosa to the platform where a big number seven hangs on a chain.

Rosa climbs the three steps, like she always does. She chooses a seat by the window, like she always does. She waves to her mother whose face is as white as a newly washed sheet. Mummy waves back briefly, her features stiff and still, and walks away, like she always does. But when the train pulls out of the station, Rosa doesn't see the fields and houses out of the window, only the remembered images of soldiers running through tangled bushes and trees, soldiers tripping up and falling, soldiers carrying their wounded friends on stretchers. She sees a soldier whose body is trapped by the branches that fell on him when the explosion ripped through his body, his helmet covering his face.

Rosa knows.

When she reaches her station, she is numb from not moving, ice-cold from sitting poker-straight and still. When she climbs off the train, she moves like a puppet with jerky limbs that don't seem to belong to her. She goes through the movements of greeting the porter who has come to meet her, of being polite, of handing over her suitcase, but inside she is empty and her heart is impossibly heavy.

* * *

It's Saturday, the day parents come to visit their children for the day or part of it. Rosa hovers outside on the path, her arms wrapped around her partly because it's cold and she's forgotten to put on her coat, partly to protect herself from the blow that is to come. She knows. She spins a bubble of invisibility around herself, not wanting to speak to anyone, not wanting anyone to speak to her, ignoring the other children who play as if nothing has happened. She walks up and down, up and down, staring into the distance, willing the car to appear, and feeling a cold dread that has nothing to do with the dank, bitter weather.

She knows.

Then her mother is here and walking towards her. She takes her daughter's hand and leads her away to a quiet spot at the edge of the gardens, away from the other children who are playing and the other children who are meeting their parents. When they are out of earshot and not observed by anyone, she lets go of her daughter's hand, bends down and wraps her arms around her.

She knows.

'Your daddy has died and you're all I've got,' Mummy says.

Rosa's mouth trembles but she doesn't cry, not here where people might see her. For a few moments, the two of them are wrapped together in private sorrow that feels like an ending.

Rosa already knows that this is the reason her mother has come to her school. She knew when she saw the soldier in the newsreel. She knew when she saw her mother's white face.

Noreen doesn't stay long. She tells her daughter she has work to do, and Rosa understands and doesn't try to keep her. Even so, the heartbreak is too big to hold inside.

'My daddy's dead,' she blurts out to the first boy she meets.

'You're a liar,' he replies.

And then the headmistress is at her side, placing an arm around her shoulders.

'Be quiet,' she tells the boy. 'It's true. Now go away and leave her alone.'

The headmistress stays with Rosa as the girl watches her mother walk away down the path.

The pain is too deep for tears, too deep for words, a dreadful ache in the very centre of her body like the feeling she had when her parents left her at Dora Russell's school when she was two and a half and she felt abandoned. She is abandoned now, in a different way, because her father is not coming home. Rosa watches the figure retreating, growing smaller, and she is proud that her mother is brave and hasn't cried in front of the other children. She vows to try her very best to be like her. She knows not to make a fuss nor to ask if she can go home with her mother because, as she tells herself, there's a war on. Mummy is busy working as an air raid warden in London. Mummy is doing important work during the Blitz. Rosa holds herself stiff and rigid, and spins a cage of steel around her small body.

That night in the dormitory, she knows the other children know that her father has died and they are waiting for her to cry and cry. Maybe they will comfort her. Maybe they are thankful it's not their father who has died. She knows they are watching and listening, tuned in to her slightest movement. She lies very still. She doesn't care about them but that's not the reason she doesn't cry. It's because she's numb and cold. Her loss is too huge for tears. Her sadness too overwhelming. Crying is pointless and futile. And yet…her daddy made a promise before he left to fight. He said when he came back from the war, he would teach her how to paint, and he said, 'We will be very happy.' Those were his last words to her before he left for war. Like a safety raft, she has clung to those words over the weeks and months and years. While she lies in her bed in the dormitory, she repeats them over and over and over and slowly the truth sinks in. Her most longed for wish will not happen. Daddy will never come home again. Daddy will never teach her to paint.

* * *

Eighteen months later, there is wild jubilation as children spill from the classrooms into the gardens and fields. They tear around the grounds, shouting and laughing. It's not playtime but they have been summoned to a special assembly and the headteacher, her voice loud, proud but trembling, has announced that the war is over. The fighting is finished. The soldiers are coming back. Girls and boys are running outside whooping with joy. After long years of fear and dread, their daddies are on their way home. Soon they will be reunited. Soon families will be whole again. Rosa turns from the overexcited children and the teachers with broad smiles on their faces and, unnoticed, walks back inside the big house and makes her solitary way to the kitchens on the floor below which she knows will be deserted. The tears she has held in like a weight of water behind a steely dam flow down her cheeks. Rivers and rivers of tears that soak her hair and dress. Leaning her head against the work counter, she sobs and sobs. The heartache is too much to bear, the loss too big to carry. She feels at breaking point and has no idea how she can mend herself. She stays in the kitchen for a long time while echoes of joy and laughter bounce down the steps from the gardens.

*I remember feeling very very brokenhearted. That is the trauma that made me an artist. A psychiatrist later told me that a trauma before puberty can get stuck. Although I'm now in my eighties, I feel that inside I am that ten-year-old girl determined to fulfil Daddy's dream. One of the best things Mummy ever said to me, just before she died, was that my father would have been very proud of me.*

## First poem
## 1944
## Age 10

What can Rosa salvage after her profound loss?

How can she live up to her father's ideals?

Can you make a ghost proud?

She'll write poetry like him, she decides, soon after Noreen brings news of his death.

The headmistress not only teaches poetry but is trying to gain a reputation as a poet herself. She doesn't look or behave like a poet, Rosa thinks, as the woman bursts into the classroom. Each lesson is the same – a hard pacing up and down at the front of the class, a poem with long words read in a loud monotonous voice from a book. Or worse, a poem she herself has written which Rosa, even at this age, knows is simply awful. It doesn't flow. The descriptions are terrible. It's flowery and too decorated. The boys aren't listening. They're throwing bits of screwed up paper at one another whenever they dare. Who wants to listen to a stupid poem? The girls try not to giggle at the boys. A few listen with concentration, including Rosa who loves words, and is interested in knowing how to make lines rhyme. *I was fascinated with how you got it to rhyme. My dad was a poet. The point is I got fascinated by it because she was talking about it, telling us how to do it, and she obviously wanted to be a poet.*

For homework, the children are told to compose a poem of their own and Rosa walks excitedly from the classroom, knowing what she wants to say. Her first chance to write a poem, like her daddy who wrote poems while he was fighting in Spain. A first opportunity to follow in his footsteps. In the classroom, she writes fast and urgently, the images and words tumbling out, the rhymes coming easily and quickly. She reads it through. It is not bad at all. With a skip of satisfaction and joy, she runs from her desk to hand in her work.

The next morning Rosa is summoned after breakfast and before class to the headmistress' office. She knocks timidly, stomach churning. What could be wrong now?

'Come in, Rosa.'

The head doesn't tell her to sit down but glares at her, waving a piece of paper that looks like the one with her poem on. Yes, it is.

'Who wrote this?' she asks.

Rosa doesn't understand the question. Nor the anger. Nor the atmosphere. Nor any of this.

'I wrote it.'

'I'll ask you again, Rosa, and this time tell the truth please. Someone wrote this for you. Who?'

'I wrote it.'

The only sound is that of nails being drummed on a hard wooden desk.

'You didn't write this. This is the work of someone quite talented. You, Rosa, are much too stupid to have written this. You only started to read a year ago. At nine! Most children can read at five.'

'But I needed glasses...'

'I don't believe that either, Rosa. I think that might have been an excuse. Perhaps you are just quite a slow child. I believe you are a stubborn, rather strange child. I believe that you also tell lies. This is another. You have handed in work that is not your own.'

Later, Rosa sheds tears in the dark corner of an empty room and vows never ever to write poetry again. She will be a painter like her daddy.

# The Blitz
# London
# Noreen
# 1944

Knowing that the war with Germany will involve the heavy aerial bombing of civilian areas, especially in London, Noreen plans ahead and arranges Rosa's life so that she is far removed from all scenes of conflict. Her plan is firm. She will arrange things so that her daughter will never see the bombs falling and never witness the carnage that is the Blitz. Holidays at home will be very short – just a few days – and Rosa will not leave the house. The uprooting and being apart for long periods is for her daughter's own safety and must be accepted. Protecting her daughter comes before the comfort of them being together. Noreen is working long hours as an air raid warden. This, after all, is what people everywhere are doing. This is the 'Blitz Spirit' of solidarity and defiance encouraged by Winston Churchill and sustained during the nation's darkest hours.

The bombs keep falling. From September 1940 to May 1941, Adolf Hitler continues his systematic attempt to bomb the British people into submission, a national ordeal which leaves deep emotional and physical scars on all who endure it. 60,000 British civilians are killed by aerial bombing. 71,000 are treated for life-threatening injuries. 88,000 are less seriously injured. In London, over one million buildings are destroyed or damaged as the most formidable air force in Europe drops its bombs across the capital. Londoners' nerves are in shreds, but their collective will to resist is not broken.

London becomes dust and rubble and wall-shattered houses displaying their intimate interiors. Did those who cooked and ate and slept in the exposed rooms survive? Did they reach the air raid shelters in time? Noreen walks the streets at night in her steel helmet, looking for any slivers of light that still leak from windows and doors and which would make the buildings dangerously illuminated magnets for the Luftwaffe criss-crossing the sky. Her job is to ensure the blackout is scrupulously maintained. London must remain unseen. Lightless. A shadow city. She is the one who sounds the air raid sirens, or if another warden has got there first, she's out on the streets, marshalling people into the shelters, making sure the old and weak are not left behind. Once she's ensured others are safely installed, she remains outside, scanning the sky for the fall of bombs within her sector and reporting the consequences to the police and ambulance crews who wait for news. Some nights, she clambers over newly fallen rubble to rescue people from bomb-shattered properties. Her work is terribly dangerous, but Noreen protects Rosa from finding out the truth about her situation.

Does she never worry about what will become of her daughter should she be killed? When the war finally ends, and the losses tallied, she will know how grave were the risks she took. 1.5 million men and women served as wardens during World War II with 127,000 working full-time at the height of the Blitz. Over two thousand of them were killed doing their duty protecting civilians.

## Handling cows and drawing horses
## 1942 – 1944
## Age 9 and 10 and 11

While Noreen walks London's streets, black and silent except for the red flares and sickening explosions where bombs fall and hit, Rosa is out of harm's way in her farm school in the country.

'Everyone here helps to look after the animals,' the headteacher tells Rosa on her first day. 'You'll have your duties on the farm which I'll hand out every morning, as well as your lessons and free time. Here we all muck in together. I hope you'll be very happy.'

Rosa lives in boots, wellies and old jumpers, is forever muddy and dishevelled, and rides with the others on top of the cart that's pulled by the tractor or pushes a wheelbarrow across windswept fields to clean or feed the animals. Trudging about in all weathers brings colour to her cheeks and makes her limbs strong. There is a freedom here that so far only Polperro has offered her, and soon she is content.

The day starts early.

'Come on,' her friend calls. 'We mustn't be late.'

Rosa runs with the other children from the annexe where they all sleep to the main hall which is echoey and very cold. There, lined up and listening, she waits to find out what her farming job is for that day.

'I hope I'm on cleaning the rabbits,' she whispers. 'I love them, all fluffy and soft. And it's easy work.'

'Me too! We all want to do the rabbits.'

'Or I'd like to milk the goats. The goats are friendly.'

'I'd rather milk the cows...oh sssh...'

The head has come in and is waiting for quiet so that he can read today's list.

'Rosa Branson.' He nods and smiles at her. 'Pigsties.'

'Oh no!' Rosa groans. 'I hate mucking out the pigs.'

'Hard luck. But don't complain. Someone has to do it and next time it won't be you.'

It's true. The rota is fair and everyone gets a turn at the easy jobs. Rosa goes off to get a shovel and rake, loads them into a wheelbarrow and trundles off down the path. A stiff easterly wind with droplets of rain whips her hair round her face and stings her cheeks. Her coat is no protection against its icy blast. In the pens though, the coat is soon shrugged off and placed over a half-door while she trudges knee-deep through muddy, filthy straw, trying to avoid the butting and rubbing of the more familiar and friendly of the pigs. The best plan is to rake the old bedding from the walls to the centre, then shovel it outside into a big smelly pile, then load it into her barrow and wheel it away to be dumped. Then return to do the same again. And again. There is pleasure in the repetition.

It's another day, another job. Rosa is mucking out the cows with a young farmhand but one of the great beasts is over-inquisitive, treads too close and nudges her.

'Hey!' she shouts, falling into the straw.

'Listen, you need to learn how to handle them,' the boy tells her, once she's back on her feet. 'There's a way of doing it so even someone small like you is safe.'

'I'm not small,' Rosa starts to complain, then shuts up. He's trying to help her.

'OK, get hold of one of its horns with your left hand. Like this.' He puts a fist around the horn of the cow who's knocked her over. 'Now gently tap its nose with your right hand. Like this.'

The cow dips its head and backs off. Moves away.

'Come on. You try with Daisy there,' the boy says. 'She's docile.'

Rosa does the same, reaching on tiptoe to grab the horn. As she bends the cow's head down and taps its nose, the cow moves slowly backwards, away from her, into a corner.

'Lesson learned. Someone should have already told you that,' the boy smiles. 'And listen, if a cow has a calf, she is likely to be more aggressive because she's protecting her baby, so either stay well clear or be very careful around her and get ready to run.'

Rosa nods. This is all interesting and she loves learning.

'And how do you behave around bulls?' the boy continues, wanting to finish Rosa's education.

'I don't think I'd grab one of their horns,' Rosa replies.

The boy laughs. 'You stay right away from bulls. Them are dangerous!'

Indoors is not so much fun because there isn't the space to run and keep warm, and keeping warm is a nagging, ever-present priority. Rosa feels the cold dreadfully, her hands and feet are clumsy lumps of ice, and shivers ripple down her body. In the main room, a fire stays lit, but all the warmth seems to remain in the grate. Rosa arrives at Springfield during a bitter January. By February, she, like all the others, has chilblains on every finger and toe from working outside without gloves and from being inside, writing words and doing sums in an unheated room. The chilblains burn and itch. The children sleep in an annexe, in dormitories, where the blankets and sheets are always damp. When Rosa lays down her weary head, she feels the cloying stickiness of her pillow.

Perhaps because of the damp and cold, Rosa's shoulder becomes painful, a dull ache that hardens to pain when she pushes the wheelbarrow or lifts heavy sacks. The doctor who calls at the school takes a look.

'You have rheumatism,' he says. 'Do they work you that hard?'

Rosa just smiles. She won't complain.

'I'll tell you what you need to cure that. At breakfast every day, you must have a heaped tablespoon of sugar.'

Expecting a bottle of nasty tasting medicine, this is music to Rosa's ears. With sugar rationing, she is the envy of the whole school. But sugar does nothing to help her rheumatism.

Despite being permanently cold, despite the chilblains and the pain in her shoulder, Rosa thrives on the hard physical toil, the closeness to the animals, and the freedom that is part of this school's ethos. Between schoolwork and farmwork, in her generous free time, she takes herself off alone to draw the horses. There's one favourite spot, half-hidden in long grass, where she is close to the animals. They come right up to the fence and tear at the spare clumps of grass. She plumps herself down, her materials close by, and spends hours lost to everything but the task she has set herself. Choosing one creature at a time, she traces the anatomy under its skin: the bones, muscles, tendons and ligaments, the many joints and connective tissue that form the skeleton that is both its framework and the protection for the soft organs beneath. The words used to describe the horse's anatomy, looked up in a book, are marvellous so she recites them as she works her way from ears to tail: poll, withers, flank, cannon, fetlock, pastern, ergot, dock. Using fine and heavy pencil strokes, she works until she has a true scaffolding on which to build the flesh and skin. Movement is harder — the toss of a head or the synchronisation of neck, back and legs as a horse walks away. How to capture that effortless fluidity? Rosa stays until her legs are all pins and needles from being folded under her and her fingers are too cold and numb to hold the pencil. Back she goes to thaw out as best she can and later to cast a critical eye over her work. This precious time alone, when she concentrates on improving her technique, is valuable and rewarding. Already, Rosa is becoming self-sufficient, relying on her own observations, and valuing the perfecting of her technique above anything she is taught in the art room. It starts here, sitting in damp grass next to a field where horses drop their fine heads to graze and move on in smooth, choreographed motion.

* * *

No-one particularly encourages her at Springfield. No-one spots and nurtures her talent. Here is Rosa, aged eleven, in the chrysalis form of the butterfly artist she will eventually become – independent, self-reliant, following her own intuitive advice and listening to her own criticism. The opinion of others, even her art teachers, is dismissed with a shrug. *'I was good in the art room. I knew how to draw.'* Here, in Rosa's memoir, is a first explicit acknowledgement, to herself, that she has skill. This is the first time we hear her confident enough to say that she can become an artist.

# Bombs and beauty
## 1944
## Age 11

It starts early this evening. It begins as a low distant rumble then, as it approaches, it hardens to a grinding, metallic roar just above them before it fades to a base-toned hum. And again. And again. It is the noise that accompanies sleep, that accompanies dreams and nightmares, a throbbing metronome of engines reverberating through the fabric of the building, down the walls, and into the floorboards. The girls, bedded down in the annexe, count the invisible, inexorable procession of planes across the night sky. They imagine the propellers whirring, the wings tilting to adjust height or direction, the undercarriage only feet from their roof, the black-helmeted German pilot in the cockpit. If one were to lose control here, over the dormitory... If one were to prematurely drop its load... Some of the girls bury their heads in their pillows to smother the cruel reality; others drift off when their counting reaches hundreds. The school is on the Luftwaffe's direct flight path to those fated, targeted areas of London where they will drop their bombs and reduce other people's bedrooms to shards of splintered wood, lumps of concrete and bloody dust. The planes of death fly on a line drawn in the sky until first light.

One morning, the girls emerge after another broken night to wander across to the main building for their breakfast, in pairs, in groups, some alone. But what is this? The pathways, the trees, the soil and the vegetation, as far as the eye can see, is draped and covered in silver, shimmering ribbons like tinsel from a hundred Christmas trees. The autumn bushes are draped in it. Flowers seem to be made of tinfoil. With each breath of wind, the electric white strands lift into the air, spin, float, dazzle and return to the earth. It is magical. It is fairyland.

The girls break ranks and run. They race across the sparkling grass and pick up the long, thin ribbons, gathering them in their arms until they too are shimmering creatures clothed in silver. They try throwing the stuff, like snowballs, but the ribbons are weightless and go nowhere. Still wreathed in the shiny foil, the girls run to the main building and race in like autumn fairies, glittering streamers winding to the floor.

There's a teacher waiting for them, smiling, expecting this entrance. She tries to restore order.

'OK, OK...please unwind all the streamers and come and put them in this sack,' she says, holding out a bag that once contained chicken feed.

'What is it?' they ask, reluctantly returning to their normal forms. 'What is it?'

'Quiet! Everyone be quiet now. I'll explain.' She waits for silence. 'It's called chaff. It's dropped from our planes to send confusing signals to the Germans' defence systems so they can't see where our planes are. It creates a cloud of false echoes. The electromagnetic equivalent of a visual smoke screen.'

The girls from Rosa's dormitory look puzzled.

'Put simply, the chaff is a decoy. Our planes hide inside the noise of signals made by these metallic streamers. Does that make sense?'

'So the planes coming over last night were British planes? To drop this stuff?' It's one of the older boys.

'Yes.'

'I heard them. They started early last night.'

There's a chorus of 'And I did' and 'And me.'

'But other nights it's the Luftwaffe.'

'Well...we are on the German flight path to London.'

'I hate the planes coming over.' A girl this time who adds, more quietly, 'They frighten me.'

'You are safe here,' the teacher replies. 'We're in an isolated house in the country. The German planes are heading for the cities.'

The German planes with their loads of bombs are heading for London where my mummy is an air raid warden, Rosa thinks, tuning out the conversation about war which sometimes rumbles in the background, like the planes rumble through the night. She moves to the window and gazes out. 'Horrible, but beautiful,' she says, to herself. 'A storm of silver.' It would be difficult to paint.

With a few nightly interludes of unearthly silence in which the girls wait, and still wait to pick up the faint but inevitable throttle noise in the east, the planes, loaded with bombs or tinsel, cross the skies above the dormitory. Winter comes and the temperature drops again. It's one of the coldest on record with ice hanging in crystal tears from the gutters and the inside glass of the windows rough and frilly with frost. Rosa's breath is icy smoke and it takes an immense effort to exit the tepid warmth of her bed. This morning she is late, partly from her reluctance to bear the cold, partly from her numb fingers' inability to push buttons through buttonholes and to tie shoelaces in knots and bows. But when she steps outside, she gasps at the transformation. The garden is crisp and hard, plants and bushes caught in frozen poses and drenched in icing sugar. Setting off, she steps on crunchy grass, breaking the film of ice that coats every blade. With her budding artist's eye, she takes in the texture of the frost, the shapes of winter and the colours that are so many shades of white. *I remember the beauty of the dewdrops on the driveway which sparkled like jewels. I used the memory of them in a painting forty years later.*

## When I grow up...
## 1945 – 1949
## Age 12 to 16

*After the war was over, my mother decided I should return to Beltane School where left-wing extremists sent their children.*

Rosa is happier back at Beltane School during her adolescent years. Decades later, she remembers them as days of possibility and some laughable failures. She samples the creative and academic subjects with enthusiasm and like most children, she considers various options for her grown-up self, trying them on for size. Do they fit? Is she comfortable in this skin? Do others encourage her or dissuade her? Some are brief flirtations that quickly fizzle out but Rosa wears each possibility seriously, like a practice run at the person she may become.

I will do something useful, she tells herself. I will work hard and not waste my time. My mummy works very hard and cares deeply about communism and helping people who are poorer than she is. Rosa has heard Noreen condemn those she calls *dilettantes*, and knows her views about the idle, pointless lives of the rich and privileged, the background she herself fled to marry Clive. Of course I will be like Mummy when I grow up, Rosa promises herself. Like both my parents.

Her mother's words accompany her every step: *'Darling, I don't mind what you do as long as you do it properly.'* Yes, art is always present, but it sometimes becomes soft focus while she lets herself consider other futures. These are the years when Rosa and her peers slowly metamorphose from children to young women.

Wednesdays bring ballet lessons taught by a retired ballerina; at Beltane only the highest standards prevail. The girls change eagerly into ballet dresses and pink slippers with long ankle ribbons. Conscious of the surprising changes in their bodies, they preen in front of the full-length mirrors that line the walls of the studio. Here are young women blossoming into womanhood, playing out their last months in children's bodies. Some are lithe and supple, some naturally well-coordinated, some will-of-the-wisp quick and light. Others are not destined to be dancers. At the bar, the most confident stretch their foal-like limbs and bend swiftly and easily from the waist to touch their toes. Following the stretching, they move to the dance floor to practise simplified routines set to classical ballet music. Rosa loves every step, every stretch and move, and in the early years commits fully to the ecstasy and liberation of movement, not passing judgement on herself or others. But as time passes, and she continues to do her very best, she must gradually acknowledge – because she is nothing if not always ruthlessly honest with herself – that the body she is growing into has neither the height nor the slenderness nor the springy lightness nor the flexibility that would offer the possibility of becoming a real ballerina. She imagines future stages in packed theatres, lit by spots, the curtain about to go up on Swan Lake, but she is not there. She is not there as the solo performer. She isn't even in the chorus. After class one day, after years of Wednesdays on the dance floor, she waits until the other girls have left and approaches the teacher, wanting a final, formal pronouncement. Honesty has always been important, a currency used by her parents from the time when she could barely walk, let alone dance. She is brave enough to want certainty.

'Excuse me,' she says, boldly.

The teacher turns and smiles, knowing that if this pupil has a question, it will be an important one.

'I'm not really very good, am I?'

The teacher pauses, searching for the right words. No, Rosa Branson does not have the physique or grace of a professional ballerina.

'You have beautiful hands,' she replies, diplomatically.

Ballet fades to enjoyable, energetic afternoons and Rosa transfers her passion to singing, after all, her mother has a formidable voice. Music at Beltane is taught by a concert pianist who gave singing lessons to opera singers before fleeing Germany. He's selective about who he takes on, but Rosa comes with credentials.

'Your mother sang in the Bach choir,' Rudi says, when Rosa turns up for her first private lesson. 'I'm happy to take you.'

'My mother plays the piano and sings,' Rosa replies, confirming her right to be there.

After she has sung some scales and a short, easy piece, Rudi looks at her with surprise. 'You have a very strong voice. This we can work on,' he tells her.

Rosa sings in the lessons, in her room, in the gardens, in the echoing corridors. In near perfect pitch. Her hopes rise. Others put their fingers in their ears.

'Rosa, my dear...'

Weeks have passed. Rosa has sung many times for Rudi and awaits his verdict. With hope and confidence.

'You have developed an absolutely enormous mezzo-soprano voice. I've rarely heard a voice that carries so far and with such force. You will make a superb Wagnerian opera singer.'

So delighted to be praised, she does not hear the very slight caveat. Wagner, but not Mozart or Puccini.

'I want you to join my German class, as well as continuing your singing lessons because some of the most famous operas are composed by Germans, and you need to know the language. You'll sing in German.'

Rosa breathes in from the depths of her powerful lungs and feels the warmth of pride. But sometimes pride comes before a fall. The German classes are hard. Rosa finds the sounds ugly but struggles on, trying to repeat and commit to memory the long strings of guttural sounds that are almost totally without meaning. In the exam, she scores minus sixteen out of one hundred. When Rudi tells her, she giggles. For some reason, she finds it funny. 'Sorry, Rosa!' she says to herself. 'I know you can draw, but I rather hoped you could be an opera singer as well.'

'Don't worry about the language,' Rudi tells her. 'Stick to singing.'

A bright operatic future singing Brünnhilde and Cosima goes the same way as her earlier fantasies about dancing Giselle and the Sugar Plum Fairy. The curtain comes down on two stage careers.

*After I left school I joined the London Youth Choir. The conductor kept telling me to be a bit quieter, and when I heard a recording I understood. Over the top was an enormous soprano voice. That was me!*

*I was told that women singers lose their voices at sixty while men continue until they are seventy. Women in my family all live into their nineties and I couldn't bear the thought of not being able to create for thirty years so I decided to be a painter instead. I'm so glad I made that decision. I'm eighty and in the last twenty years have done my best work on a large scale.*

As if the truth will finally out, Rosa's way forward is illuminated with light bulbs that flare brightly instead of flickering and going out.

'We have a different art teacher this term,' a friend tells her one day. 'He's called Arthur Wragg but everyone calls him Raggy.'

Rosa shrugs. 'My father was a real artist. I doubt any teacher can be as good.'

'Raggy is a real artist too.'

'But that means nothing. There are good and bad artists.'

'And he's a socialist and a pacifist.'

Rosa finally pays attention, and looks forward to her first art lesson.

And art lessons take a very different turn when, at last, the teacher is a painter whom Rosa likes and respects. Wanting his pupils to understand the human form, Wragg sets up a life class with girls taking turns to pose in bathing suits. Rosa enjoys herself, one of very few who understand the importance of anatomy, because without the solid structure beneath how can one possibly draw the soft flesh on top? Her horses at Springfield Grange have stood her in good stead. The teacher wanders round, making helpful comments and suggestions. Beside Rosa's easel, he always stops and nods.

'Good,' he says. 'The form is good.'

Half way through the term, she comes to class wearing her bathing suit because, according to the rota, it's her turn to be the model. She's draped a big towel over her shoulders for modesty and to try to keep warm. There will be an hour of staying very still and getting very cold.

'No, Rosa,' Raggy says, when he arrives in the classroom and sees her standing there. 'No, no! Run back and put your ordinary clothes back on, then come and join the others. You're too good at art to waste your time posing.'

He instructs a less fortunate soul and presumably a lesser artist to run quickly and put on a swimsuit. Rosa's heart almost bursts with pride. Someone, a respected artist even, has told her she is good at art. She can't remember any other time, in all her art lessons, in all her schools, when a teacher has singled her out like this for praise.

Rosa has held her wish to be a proper artist like her father close to her heart and has carried it secretly through discouragement and disapproval, as well as fleeting considerations of other ways to spend her life. Now, like the first layer in a painting that follows the technique of the Old Masters, she can palely sketch in a future life which, though still in shadow form, is composed and intact. She will build on this, layer by layer.

More approval unfolds. Rosa is asked to paint a mural for the end of term dance. It will be her first oil painting, of three ladies, and is considered enough of a success to be exhibited on a wall where the best of the pupils' art is displayed.

This painting, among others, helps her get a place at Camberwell Art College.

# 7 ON LONELINESS, ANGER AND DIPLOMACY

An extract from an interview
Rosa
2017


WAS ALL YOUR childhood lonely?

*I felt lonely until I was sixteen and went to art school. And then I met all these people who became friends.*

So up to sixteen you were aware you were different? You didn't fit in?

*That's right. I didn't fit in.*

In what way?

*They were all bossy and chucking their weight around.*

Were they confident?

*They were aggressive so you learned to be a diplomat.*

So in order not to be bullied, you discovered behaviour that would not annoy them? So they didn't pick on you?

*Yes. That's right.*

It sounds like a sad childhood.

*Well, it is. It very often is for kids at boarding school but it turned me into a diplomat so when you meet some aggressive bloke, thumping everyone, you don't oppose him or he'll thump you. You tell him how strong he is! Diplomacy!*

How did you enact that diplomacy?

*I remember one bloke who was being horrible and I hit him and he hit me in the face and made my nose bleed. So then I started to think how I could get round it. If they're boasting about something, and you don't know how to do it, you tell them how clever they are.*

But that's hard to do as a child.

*Yes but it's quite handy for later.*

Did you use that later on as an artist?

*I still do.*

How are you using it?

*Well, when I meet artists who are doing appalling work, I'm very kind to them. I say, 'Oh you're a very creative gentleman.' It's a pile of rubbish really but you don't aggressively fight them, you don't do that, you don't make anyone unhappy because then they just fight back.*

What did you do with your unhappiness?

*Put it in a painting.*

But that was later.

*No, I did it from the age of seven. I painted. When I was unhappy, I used art to get round it.*

From an early age were you retreating into your drawing in order to cope with being lonely?

*Yes.*

Was it defensive or was it also a creative thing?

*Well, it was creative. It's the creative use of negative energy. If somebody is horrid to you, you paint them as the devil and I still do it. That lady climbing up those steps* (points at a painting) *is the devil climbing up those steps. That's the lady from The Salvation Army. You've got your own back! And I painted that devil climbing up the steps because that was the lady who told everyone I was painting people to mortify them, and my friend was furious and my daughter, Peggy, was furious. I was painting this picture and I came and said to my students, 'This is the lady from The Salvation Army. It's not doing her any harm because it doesn't actually look like her. Nobody knows except me.' I've been doing it ever since.*

It's an interesting mixture of what you talked about earlier of emotion and technique.

*Yes. You use it. And you can't paint the devil unless you actually know how to paint bats' wings. I mean this is what you do. And because you do it properly, it's very powerful.*

And does this dispel your personal feelings?

*Yes, you think it's funny.*

The aggression is turned into humour. The hurt is turned into humour?

*Exactly. I started doing that when I was seven. The kids were teasing me at school and I drew the kids and made them look horrible and the matron came in and said, 'What lovely drawings,' and I thought, 'You don't know what you're talking about. I was the one in control.'*

I'm seeing and hearing two Rosas. The strong one almost from the beginning because of her father and knowing about communism and knowing that her mother is a very strong person and wanting to go through life being strong...

*That's right.*

...but I'm also seeing the sad lonely child. How do they fit together?

*Isis. Isis had two sides. She had the creativity and she had the organisation. Put them together and you've got Michelangelo. Don't put them together and you've got an alcoholic.*

If you hadn't had the painting, the technique, the visual creativity, you might have crumbled? Do you think you would?

*Yes. I would have been one of those despairing people who...yes, of course I would.*

An interesting question then, are all creative people like that?

*A lot of them are. It's the same thing.*

Because to be creative you have to have a thin skin? You have to be open to feelings?

*I KNOW YOU DO! And you don't ignore them! You use them!*

But you are also vulnerable.

*Well, you are. But you learn how to use those feelings. Many people have been brought up in comfortable, cosy families and whenever they're feeling depressed, Mum will come along and support them and then they don't know how to do it for themselves. This is the point. If you haven't had that support, then you have to learn to fight on your own and that comes in very handy because you don't then lean on people. You stand on your own feet and I've taken it to the extent where I'm bloody crazy.*

Rosa roars with laughter.

# 8 THE ART STUDENT

**Three lectures
Camberwell Art College
1952
Age 19**

TODAY THREATENS TO be a dull day, an old-fashioned, waste of time kind of day, at least so most of the students assume. They are bored before the lecture even begins and ask why these three lectures have been included in their curriculum. Dr Ruhemann, a restorer at the National Gallery, is about to arrive to show them how to paint in the style of Rubens. What for? they ask. Haven't we moved on from Rubens and others of his era? They might as well teach us Latin!

While others barely conceal their boredom, wanting only to get back to work on their own exciting compositions, Rosa is alert and anxious, a tight ball of nervous energy which she tries to damp down in case her hopes are again dashed. After the hours spent miserably aiming blobs of colour at her canvas in a reluctant imitation of Cézanne, she will see an expert paint in the style she adores and admires. Here he comes, a faint smile on his lips, looking round at his audience as if anticipating a tepid response, and not minding in the least. He gives a brief introduction, setting his practice in its historical context. The canvas on the easel is ready-stretched and prepared. Ruhemann mixes oils and paints, dips his brush and begins, all the time talking animatedly about the technique he is using, explaining how it is all about layers. Layer upon layer upon layer. It is the complete antithesis of the right-first-time daubs of paint technique taught at Camberwell and it is music to Rosa's ears. While some students have started to doodle on their drawing pads, clearly not listening, not watching, not making notes, Rosa hangs eagerly on Ruhemann's every word, follows every brushstroke and sees with a hesitant joy how the painting's composition takes its faded but whole and intact shape on the blank space. Rosa knows that this is the style she needs to learn. 'Yes!' she says to herself. 'Yes! This is how I want to paint. This is the right way to paint. This is the only way to paint. I don't care if I am the only student in this entire art school who wants to paint the modern world using this wonderful old technique. I am sure. I have been sure since I was a child.'

The flashback comes again, and with the same painful sharpness. A mother takes her little girl by the hand and stops in front of paintings by Rubens and Rembrandt in the National Gallery. Rosa remembers it as if it were yesterday. She is six years old. She is back there, staring with great concentration and voicing a secret promise to herself. And for her beloved father. *I looked up at the wonderful paintings of Botticelli and Titian and Leonardo and I thought, 'When I grow up I will do pictures like this.'*

Today, Rosa watches Dr Ruhemann use raw sienna to sketch the pale outline of the composition, a ghost of the painting to come. 'Imprimatura,' he tells his audience, 'is the name for this first layer which is semi-transparent or a transparent colour base which creates the background for the painting. It's a harmonising element for the colour layers that follow and determines the darkness or lightness of the composition. The white background beneath reflects the light through the imprimatura and semi-transparent layers, creating an almost magical three-dimensional illusion.' Of course, he tells the students with a smile, he can't in three lectures create anything close to a painting by Rubens, but he can show them the technique which all the Old Masters used. What he can offer them are the tools of the trade. Rosa is nodding her head, her heart racing in acknowledgement as she hears what she has been longing to hear. She will find a way to learn this technique, this vital, essential way of painting which Camberwell has failed to show her.

There are a few empty chairs and lame excuses for Dr Ruhemann's second lecture, but he is no fool, and knows he is preaching mainly to the unconvertible. Rosa is already there, in her seat at the front, notebook in hand, not that she writes a word because all she needs are her eyes on the canvas.

'Hello,' Dr Ruhemann says. 'You're an early bird. Are you interested?'

'I want to paint like the Old Masters,' Rosa replies without prevarication. 'I'm more than interested. I'm desperate to learn the correct technique so that I can paint properly. They have taught me nothing here.'

Taken aback at this young woman's passion and despair, he says, 'Well, I'm sure you've learned something here, but if you're keen on knowing about Rubens and the other Old Masters you've come to the right place.'

Once the stragglers have arrived, Dr Ruhemann starts painting on top of the shadowy form of the previous week, explaining about the second layer of underpainting which is done with burnt or raw sienna, darker than the first layer but still without colour. 'The imprimatura should still be slightly visible through the darkest parts,' he explains. 'We don't add in the small details yet and areas where we'll paint bright reds or bright blues are also left uncovered.'

Rosa sighs her relief because here is a technique that flies completely in the face of the blobs and splatters of colour she's been throwing at her canvas during her time at Camberwell. What she is seeing now is the painstaking building of the scaffolding that will underpin the whole painting in shadow form. It will lie in wait for the colour and detail. If the structure isn't right, the painting will fail. This is how it should be, Rosa thinks. The style is oddly familiar and absolutely right, like something she knew in another life but has since lost. There has never been any question about how Rosa wants to paint. Dr Ruhemann's voice brings her back to the urgent present.

'Of course if I were Rubens, and I clearly am not, this would be a lengthy process as he considers the composition and builds layer after layer, letting each dry, and maybe going over some, but in three lectures I'm taking shortcuts so the finished painting will be rather basic, but you will, at least, be able to see the process.'

'So the colour always comes later?' Rosa asks, unable to contain her eagerness. 'After the layers that are almost transparent?'

'Yes. I'll do some of the colour layers after we've had a break, and this second transparent layer has had a chance to dry. Of course it should dry for a lot longer, but you'll just have to imagine that if I were Rubens, a lot more time would have passed before I did anything more.'

After the painting of the next layers, the students troop out, a few not bothering to return, but Rosa remains in her seat, intently studying the partly finished painting. Dr Ruhemann stays too, drinking tea from a flask and eating sandwiches. He has worked out by now that the serious pupil in the front row is neither a popular nor a highly regarded student and feels curiosity and compassion. If intensity makes an artist, she's already there, but he has nothing else on which to form an opinion. Certainly she's watching him as if her life depends on it. He tries to ignore her until the lecture resumes.

'In the next stage,' he continues, once most of the students have trooped back, 'which, as I've explained, I'm rather rushing, but you'll get the gist of it, only four colours are used: lead or titanium white, yellow ochre, red ochre and bone or ivory black. The trick now is to mix them so that you have a scale of neutral greys. First mix black and white, then add a bit of yellow ochre. Add red ochre carefully until it eliminates the greenishness brought to the mixture by the yellow. Paint thickly in the light areas and thinly in the shadows. Don't use semi-transparent, soapy layers. Leave a small percentage of the darkest parts of the shadows uncovered.'

He pauses to catch up with his own instructions, to mix his paint, and to apply the grey tones. Some students fidget, finding the whole business dull beyond words. Rosa is ecstatic as she watches this building of a painting from its complete and beautifully composed raw sienna composition to its final colours and detail. The completeness of it, even at the very start, is utterly compelling. And right. This is the right way to paint. She knows.

'By the end, the objects on your painting should look like they are made out of unpolished marble without details in the highlighted areas and the darkest shadows,' Dr Ruhemann says, putting down his brush. 'We'll leave it here until next week when I'll show you the highlighting and final details.'

Students are already rising to leave. Rosa moves from her chair to the easel, and looks close up at the half-finished work. All is smooth and exact. The wholeness is astonishing.

'It's wonderful,' she says. 'This is how I want to paint. Not using the alla prima technique they make us use here. I don't know how to paint shadows. I can't paint light.'

'It's not popular anymore. Gone out of fashion,' Dr Ruhemann replies. 'I'm only here as a kind of historian, showing students what painters did during the Renaissance, and then they can go back to painting like Cézanne. I can see they can't wait to get shot of me. It's the same every year.'

'I don't want to paint like Cézanne. What do you truly think of the technique of the Old Masters?' Rosa holds her breath while she waits for the reply.

'I think the technique is brilliant. I wouldn't be teaching it if I didn't admire it. I wouldn't be working as a restorer of paintings in the National Gallery either. It's my passion.' He studies the earnest, unhappy face hanging on his every word and sees a truly troubled spirit. 'If you're not happy with the way you've been taught here, then go somewhere else. If this is how you want to paint, then copy the great painters of the past in the National Gallery. Camberwell isn't the answer for every student.'

Rosa glances up at this wonderful man who is offering her a flicker of hope.

'Thank you,' Rosa replies. 'I'll look forward to your next lecture.'

'I'll be painting the darkest colours and the highlights.'

'Can you please explain that to me now. I know you'll show us, but

I'm eager to know.'

Impossible to resist this girl's hunger for knowledge. And does he sense in Rosa a creative talent that has hit a painful barrier?

'You use ultramarine, Prussian blue, madder lake deep, red cinnabar or cadmium red, cadmium or lead yellow. You must match the shade of darkness to those in the previous layer so one step lighter for highlighted areas and one step darker for shadows. Each time, narrow the highlighted and shadow areas, painting them lighter or darker.'

'I understand.'

'And then come the highlights.'

'The light?'

'Yes, the miraculous light you see glowing from a Titian or a Rembrandt.'

'I haven't found a way to paint light. I can't paint the light in my mother's eyes or the glow of candlelight in a copper jug or the shimmer of sunset on water. I have no idea how to do it.' Rosa sighs, distraught at the prospect of not knowing.

And Dr Ruhemann hears her despair, but stays firmly, evenly on course. 'It's all in the layers. You add the highlights last, on top of the rest. You'll see next time, if I can get to the finishing line. The thing is, if this were a real painting, by a real painter from that era, there would be many, many more layers and I won't be able to show you those. I'm cutting a lot of corners doing it in three lectures.'

'You've shown me enough,' Rosa says. 'And you've given me some hope. Thank you.' She knows intuitively that she must not impose further on this kind man.

He watches the figure walk away and wonders what it must be like to be out of step with the style of painting adopted by everyone else around her. To be the odd one out. Perhaps he's pleased to find a student who is genuinely interested in the technique he teaches because there certainly aren't many. Or does he recognise in Rosa a young artist whose desire to paint comes from her very heart and soul, but who is wise enough to know that passion isn't enough and that she will fail unless she finds the right way to paint? Still thinking about Rosa, he bends down to pack up his things.

Only for a brief time can Rosa keep the flame of hope alive. It may be possible to start again, she tells herself. But back in the studio, she stares with hatred at her half-finished, splattered painting that has no shadows and no light, and is distraught. Classes continue with Ruhemann's three lectures fading to a brief and tantalising interlude in a curriculum she loathes.

*I saw the chap from the National Gallery. I saw him give three lectures when I was at Camberwell and he painted a Rubens in three lectures and I thought, 'That's what I want to know. Right!' He knew how to do it because he'd been a painter in Berlin and he got so fascinated with how the Renaissance had done it, building them up, that he became the great restorer of the Berlin Museum, Dr Ruhemann. Then Hitler came to power so he fled to England. He was teaching in the National Gallery, teaching young people how to be restorers.*

## On the bridge in Regent's Park
## 1953
## Age 20

It is evening and the light is fading. Rosa, face set like stone, stops at the bridge over the canal in Regent's Park on her way home from Camberwell Art College and looks down at the slow-moving water littered with fallen autumn leaves. Willows dip their branches and add tiny green diamonds to the floating reds and golds. The London sky is bruised and inflamed, its colours reflected in a disarray of lines and fragile shapes that break and shift each time the breeze lifts. Light and shade shift and reform.

This is exactly what Rosa longs to paint in its full glorious colour with defining shadows and teasing light. Or rather, longed to paint. Today she sees only the reality of the place, not its promise of transformation into a painting. She has no desire to paint. She can't paint. Her joy and enthusiasm and dedication have been crushed and bruised. She hasn't painted for three weeks and when she doesn't paint, depression and despair crawl into her soul and plunge her into desolation.

It's a long drop from the bridge to the water and Rosa can't swim. In her imagination she feels the short fall followed by the shocking slap as her body hits the surface, then sinks into the mud and slime below. If she jumps, it will be over. If she leans over the railings a bit further, bending from the waist, hanging her head forwards and tipping her weight until gravity seizes and pulls her, then there will be no going back and that will be the end of it. How else to break this tension and lack of resolution?

She has spent three futile, disappointing years at Camberwell, wanting with a fierce desire to create real art and finding no-one who will show her how to do it. She carries around the memory of her mother taking her, aged six, to the National Gallery and showing her paintings. 'Your daddy says these are the greatest painters in the world,' she said. Rosa remembers looking up at them and thinking, how will I ever do it?

She had such high hopes of Camberwell. She would find there real art taught by real artists and would learn the techniques of the Old Masters. Instead, she has to paint in blobs and smatterings, loading her brush time after time with the exact colour and swiping it on the canvas with a single stroke. If the colour is wrong, she has to scrape it off, re-mix the tone and throw the paint again. *We were told you shouldn't put the shadows in because it's old-fashioned. You shouldn't paint in layers, you shouldn't use any sable brushes, you ought to be able to see the proper brushstroke because this was how you expressed your feelings. You weren't supposed to paint beauty because it was chocolate-boxy, but you were allowed to paint Camberwell Green in the rain, or the dustbins, because this showed integrity.* Rosa paints skies that are spotted and skin that is blotched. Where are the warm blended tones of real flesh? Where is the light and shade that marks the contours of a human face? Where are the ridges and troughs of a human hand?

For three frustrating, confusing years, she goes through the motions of studying art without feeling any emotional connection to what she is doing. Or worse, she does what she is told while knowing that she is painting in a style that kills stone dead her wish to paint the world as she wants to paint it.

Only once did she find the courage to ask if she could paint in a different way.

'You mean like the Old Masters?' her tutor repeated, incredulous. 'You're at Camberwell, Rosa. We teach the techniques of the modern, experimental painters. Why go backwards to the heavy dark paintings of Rembrandt and...'

'Rembrandt isn't dark. His paintings glow with light and I want to know how to paint that light.'

'Cézanne paints light. Don't you think his colour balance is exciting? Every single brushstroke relates to the previous brushstrokes and builds part of what he sees. What looks at first glance like a daub is intentional and integrated.'

'I don't want to paint daubs.'

Rosa's eyes brim with tears – tears of frustration and tears of rage with the quick-fire blobs she's been throwing with a simmering rage at her canvas. She'd like to shake her loaded paintbrush all over this benighted tutor. All over the damn floor. That's where the pointless splodges belong.

At the railings, she relives the utter futility of painting in a style that she hates and despises. Goodness, she has tried. Her memories of tutors' instructions and admonitions, and lately their disdain and dismissal, crowd out the click and thud of people's footsteps passing her on the bridge. One or two people turn to wonder why a beautiful young woman is leaning over the railings, her face a mask of misery, staring at the water below.

– 'You must never use a sable brush.'

– 'No, layers are wrong. You aim for one correct brushstroke. Repeat it. Repeat and repeat.'

– 'You're to paint reality. Forget all thoughts of beauty and romanticism and concentrate on what's in front of you. Transform that reality in quick, short, accurate strokes.'

She remembers asking a teacher how, in this style, she is supposed to paint twenty women running down a road and is told, 'You can't.'

Rosa thinks of the light shining in her mother's eyes when she talks about her political work. She thinks of sunsets. She thinks of hands with their wells of shadows which she's not allowed to draw except with a single hard line that makes them into a cartoon instead of a shaded study of warm flesh. She thinks of landscapes composed only of multicoloured spots and asks herself how, just how, is she supposed to create a sense of space? She sighs deeply, thinking about her despised series of paintings of overflowing dustbins and Camberwell in the rain while her tutor rants on about integrity.

And what about the visions she has been having since a small child – those glorious, shimmering, multicoloured sightings of people who appear in unexpected places and exotic animals that lurk in bushes and leap from flowers and trees? They are vital to her sense of who she is and how she paints and she will not dissect and destroy them, dissolving their vitality in daubs and splashes. So here she is, after three years studying art, with not a clue how to bring those visions to life. She remembers being seven years old and seeing the gorgeous tiger with the flaming red eyes in the rhododendron bushes. She remembers running inside and telling the other children, breathless with excitement. That tiger was absolutely real to her, a breathing, living presence with its animal musk and warmth. Rosa smiles at the memory, and of the other visions that take her by surprise in the street or in a shop, or wandering around a park. There's no predicting when or where they'll appear.

From the bridge, she can see the large detached house overlooking Regent's Park where she and her mother now live. It's owned by a friend, the bottom half rented to Noreen. Leaning back to a safer and more balanced position on the bridge, her hands firmly gripping the railings, she imagines the impact of her death on her mother. A knock on the door. A policeman standing on the step, face severe, when Noreen opens it. The news, grimly revealed, that her daughter's body has been found in the canal. Drawing in a sharp breath, she knows she can't inflict that pain. Noreen has already lost her husband. To lose an only daughter too? Rosa sighs. She lifts her head and steadies herself.

'OK, Rosa,' she says, though not loud enough that people will hear her and think her insane, though she wonders if perhaps she is, 'you have to learn how to paint properly and be a real artist.' An idea takes shape as she stands there in the encroaching darkness. 'Right! I will go and draw portraits for seven hours a day in a Lyons tea shop. Every two hours I can have a cup of tea.' The plan is made. Rosa removes her hands from the railings and walks on.

*I left Camberwell more depressed than I had ever been. I was having visions and had no idea how to paint them. I remember standing on a bridge and choosing between killing myself and finding out how to paint properly. I thought, 'I can't kill myself because Mummy will be upset so I have to be a real painter.'*

## Portraits in a Lyons tea shop
## 1953
## Age 20

Through the dismal rain, and only partly protected by her loose mackintosh, Rosa strides out, clutching her bag with her sketchbook, pencils and charcoal. Across the park, she heads for the busy main road where she will spend her day in Lyons tea shop on Camden High Street. Today. Tomorrow. The next day, and the next day. For as long as it takes. In her pocket, she has money for two cups of tea.

At the door, just before she reaches for the handle, she senses a presence at her side. There's nobody there, and yet there is something, a shiver of movement, a disturbance of the air.

'Daddy?' she asks, so quietly that no-one can hear and send her to the asylum.

It can't be the wind because this morning there is none, the rain falling in straight vertical sheets, and anyway the breath that raises the hairs on her neck is neither damp nor cold.

'Daddy?' she asks again.

If an answer comes, it is faint and far away. Like a whisper, like a mirage, like a smile. 'Yes, I was here before you.'

Of course. Clive Branson was here before her, perfecting his drawing technique as a preparation for portrait painting, sitting for hours and hours in Lyons tea shops in Battersea. The daughter follows in her adored father's footsteps. The ghost – if it is a ghost – flows with her through the door and breathes at her side until she settles. Then he is gone, the exact moment marked by a small shift in the temperature of the room and in the texture of the air.

Rosa lets her ghost go. Tuning in to the tea shop, her artist's eye registers the steamy atmosphere as damp umbrellas and wet coats drip against tables and over chairs. The damp outside penetrates the interior, like swirling fog. She sees how packed the room is, and how fast the waitresses are bringing out laden trays. No wonder these institutions became popular after the war. The art deco interiors are interesting and welcoming. The waitresses are forever brisk and cheerful in their neat uniforms. The cakes and scones are reliably good. Into these tea shops, people flock for an hour or two of friendly company, for meetings, for a solitary break. Rosa is the odd one out, coming here for the whole day to meet nobody.

Good, the corner seat is being vacated by two still-chatting women and Rosa makes a beeline for it. She throws herself on the padded bench, takes off her damp hat and coat, and unpacks her drawing materials. They, at least, are dry. Some days, when the place is crowded, she has to take a temporary seat at a table in the middle where the light is too bright and the people around her too close, and she herself is far too exposed. Only with her back to the wall, and half-hidden in the relative gloom of her corner, does she feel invisible enough to give up the pretence of being like the other customers. The waitresses know and accept her. No-one

*Drawings in a Lyons tea shop*

126

objects to a young woman who spends her days drawing when she does it discreetly and with such dedication. She allows herself a cup of tea every two hours. Having been told by Gilbert Spencer, head of painting at Camberwell that women can't be artists because they don't have the physical strength to paint for six hours a day, she has set herself the target of sketching for seven hours and will stick to it. It takes stamina, and at first she droops home exhausted, but she gradually builds on her initial two hours like an athlete training for a sport until she can keep going all day.

Today, like every day, she is spoilt for choice. Over there is an elderly couple sitting in comfortable near silence over a spread of iced cakes. Next to them is a young mother with two children who has, perhaps, escaped the rained-in confines of her home, but is still fully on duty, keeping her restless children in their chairs and on their best behaviour. Or how about the young office worker sitting alone and barely lifting his eyes from his cup of tea? She could draw his shyness in his stiff, bent-over posture and in the worry lines across his forehead. Further away is a very pretty young woman in a fancy hat gossiping with three friends, clearly aware, by her slightly exaggerated movements and roaming eyes, of her attractiveness in this place crowded with others who are more ordinary. Rosa's attention moves on and lingers on the older man in a suit who is flirting with the waitress, his hand brushing her skirt when she bends to put his tea and scones on the table, and whose eyes follow her shapely form when she moves away, her posture perfect, even while balancing her tray. Yes, Rosa will start on that one and make sure the lust and longing in the man's eyes and his nervous hand movements sing from her pencil strokes.

It is vital that the people Rosa is drawing remain unaware that she is doing so. She wants to capture natural expressions and ordinary postures, not people whose self-consciousness turns them into frozen, unnatural mannequins, on red alert in case they let their shoulders slouch or they spill their tea. Such a person would completely defeat her purpose of sketching real life with all its flaws and failings, its quirkiness and blemishes. If somebody looks up and catches her drawing, she instantly looks straight past them as if she is staring hard at somebody else. The strategy usually works.

Does Clive return to look over Rosa's shoulder as she sits drawing day after day in that crowded café that echoes with the clatter of cutlery and crockery, scraped chairs and chatter, fortified only by self-rationed cups of tea? Is part of her motivation the knowledge that she is following in his footsteps? Is she tuned in to the synchronicity? Does Rosa sense his shadow falling over her table when she picks up her pencil? Does she see the slight stir of air that could be a nod of a head, an acknowledgement as she finishes a sketch. If she does, she greets it with a secret, quiet rapture.

The long days make her back ache, her eyes sore and she comes home too exhausted to do anything but fling herself in a chair and read. To compensate though, she is beginning to understand the basic techniques of drawing and the absolute necessity of practice. In a Lyons tea shop, she is closer to the chalk face of art than she had been painting blobs at Camberwell College. There is a satisfaction in that knowledge.

The long, tiring days are not in vain. Some of the later paintings based on her Lyons tea shop drawings are exhibited in the Royal Academy's Summer Exhibition, and she makes her very first sale to the actor, Rod Steiger. A painting based on a sketch of ladies sipping tea earns her a place at the Slade.

Rosa tells this anecdote complete with a mock cockney accent.

*Did I tell you about the lady who came up to me in a fury? Well, I was drawing an old lady sitting opposite me actually and suddenly another lady came from the other side of the room and shouted at me.*

*'Bloody cheek! I don't say you could draw my photo!'*

*'I'm not drawing your photo,' I said.*

*She said, 'Oh!' and went away.*

*Then the old lady said, 'You weren't drawing her photo, were you? You were drawing mine.'*

# The Slade: the Etching Room
## 1953
## Age 20

The Slade holds the illusion of promise. After the demoralising, depressing years at Camberwell which reduced her to tears of frustration and, more than once, a decision to walk away, Rosa finishes the course on the higher notes of the commissioned mural and the oil painting that grants her a place at the illustrious Slade. Few are considered good enough to apply; fewer still get in. She appreciates this acknowledgement of her talent, but a deeper joy and purpose burns more brightly than her success.

'I'll be studying where Daddy studied,' she tells Noreen, not once but several times, her excitement overflowing.

'I know, darling, and he would be very proud of you.'

'He loved the Slade, didn't he?'

'Yes. He spoke highly of it.'

'Daddy was a brilliant painter.'

'I know, darling. I wish he were here to see you following in his footsteps.' Noreen's voice doesn't waver.

'I do too. He said he would teach me to paint.'

'I remember.'

'He promised me. He said we'd be very happy and he would teach me to paint.' Rosa turns her head to hide the tears that bubble up too easily whenever her father is strongly present in their conversations.

Noreen sighs and adds the expected response. 'I know.' This memory, this promise, recalled again and again by her daughter, is perhaps coloured a tone too bright. It has taken on a towering significance. She worries sometimes that Clive's words are imprinted in her daughter's heart as if scorched there with a hot iron. She was so young, so impressionable when he died. He is forever young, forever a hero. And she adored him. They both adored him.

'I hope they'll teach me the techniques I need,' she says. 'Daddy's technique was excellent. I don't want to paint like him, but I want to be as good as he was.'

Noreen knows this exchange by heart, and while unable to advise Rosa about painting techniques, she understands her uncompromising wish to do only her very best. Perhaps she and Clive are responsible for instilling that in her.

'Rosa, do you remember what I said to you when you told me that you didn't want to be an opera singer? You were at Springfield and you came to me and said you'd changed your mind. You wanted to be a painter.'

'Of course I remember. And you said, "Rosa I don't care what you do as long as you do it *properly*."'

'Exactly. So now you have your chance. You'll learn to paint properly. I hope the Slade is all that you wish, and now I must get on with my writing. We can talk again later.'

\* \* \*

*It is no different.*

It takes only days at the Slade for Rosa to be dealt a desperate blow. To have her hopes dashed a second time is more damaging than the first time around. Against all her expectations, she is taught to paint using exactly the same techniques she struggled with and rejected at Camberwell. Surrounded by other willing and accommodating students, Rosa stands in front of her easel, teeth gritted, her brush loaded with paint and flings it on to the canvas. Blob after blob. Aim for perfection with the first swipe, she is told, or scrape it off and start again. And don't complain that you can't see what the composition is when you stand close up. Take several steps back, look from a distance, and then you'll see it in all its impressionistic glory. You'll see its integrity.

*The same rubbish.*

Rosa sleepwalks through her first term lost, bewildered, and very much alone in her rejection of all that is taught and revered. Around her, students experiment with their own versions of the approved style, painting in ways that excite them but which leave Rosa cold. For her, each aimless week, each pointless month, is like crossing a salt marsh that drags her to a standstill. Or worse – she is sucked under, unable to save herself. Anyway, why struggle to carry on? There's nothing for her out there. How, she asks herself for the hundredth time, is she supposed to learn to paint properly? She is twenty, for heaven's sake, and no nearer knowing. She hasn't even begun.

During that first term, before the starburst collision of like-minded souls that is her meeting with Alan, she is rescued only once. The escape is temporary and transient, but welcome nevertheless. Her course includes a module in traditional etching, and Rosa revels in the physicality of the work, more craft than art, and the closeness and involvement with her materials – something she will continue to use and love throughout her career. She has no preconceived ideas or expectations to block her and she is eager to learn. Apron on, sleeves rolled up, Rosa gets right down to it, loving the exertion and energy required, not minding her blackened hands and the smudges she transfers to her arms and face.

Today, having been shown the separate stages, the students have been set free to make an etching using their own designs, from start to finish. It will take at least a week, waiting between sequential processes. First, she prepares her steel plate by rubbing it evenly with wax. The surface must be smooth with no part left exposed. Rosa smooths her hands over the plate, satisfied with its sticky finish. With her design beside her, she uses a pointed etching needle to scratch the wax and expose the metal where she wants her lines to be visible in the finished piece. For more swollen lines, she uses an échoppe, a tool with a slanted oval section. The work is painstaking, built up line by single line, each accurately and cleanly cut, a negative imprint of the finished piece.

The plate is heavy but wearing protective gloves, she can lift it and drop it into the bath of acid, leaving it there until the acid bites into the metal and dissolves the parts exposed by the lines. Any lines not cleanly cut will be blurred and messy, the result unsatisfactory, but Rosa has been fastidiously careful. When she lifts out the plate and cleans off the residue, she can see that her design is almost perfect. Now to flood the plate with ink, making sure it runs deeply into the etched lines so none are left empty. Finally she wipes away all the excess, leaving only the ink's stain in the etched lines, and all over her hands and face. Rosa is a messy worker.

The hard graft and the sweet simplicity of the process are immensely satisfying. The exact cutting of line after line, the pouring and rubbing of wax and ink, the rubbing and polishing takes her far from her habitual worries. At the end of each day in the Etching Room, Rosa is tired and happy. Eager to get on with the next stage.

Towards the end of the week, Rosa bounds into the Etching Room, eager to see what she has made. She takes a large sheet of paper and moistens it to soften it slightly so that it will pick up more ink. The excitement is almost too much. Other students wetting their paper are as keen as she is and here, in the Etching Room, she is not out of tune with the communal eagerness that fills the room. She places her plate and her sheet of paper in the high-pressure printing press and waits for the paper to pick up the ink from the etched lines.

Her first etching is rather fine. It's a portrait and she appreciates the way this process of wax and ink and acid offers her a finished piece that is very precise, and a very far cry from the dispiriting daubs of her paintings. Rosa has a stack of portraits from her time in the Lyons tea shop and decides to reproduce them in this new medium. The prospect gives her a purpose and something to look forward to. There is, after all, a temporary way out of the salt marshes that threaten to pull her under.


## The Slade and the National Gallery
## 1954
## Age 21

'Ah, Rosa... Would you mind coming along with me to my office for a moment, please.'

It's Professor Coldstream, the man who was her father's best friend when he was at the Slade. He stops her in the corridor and Rosa wonders if she's in for another lecture about her negative attitude. These days she barely conceals her contempt for the way she is being taught, and people have noticed. They see she has more or less given up. 'Who cares?' she says under her breath. Her mood is very dark. Scowling, she plods along after him.

'Come in, come in. Sit down.'

He sounds cheerful, not angry. Rosa plonks her folders and bag on the floor and looks up.

'Let me get straight to the point. You know that the Slade has an arrangement with the National Gallery so that we send some of our students to copy the paintings...'

'Yes! I applied,' Rosa interrupts.

'Well, I'm coming to that. You're the only student in your year who has applied. Obviously the others don't see any point.'

'I do. I think it's terribly important.'

'So standing for hours copying old paintings appeals to you?' he asks with just a hint of sarcasm. She is, after all, his friend's daughter.

Appeals to her? How can he even ask!

'Yes!' Rosa replies. 'I'd love to do that. There's nothing I'd like more.'

'Fine. Consider it done then. You can spend one or two days a week there, and buy yourself some comfortable shoes.'

She ignores his patronising tone. The anticipation bubbles up, wave after wave, and as she retraces her footsteps back to the studio, she gives a little skip of joy. She has been given permission to do what she wants to do. How long has she waited for this moment? This absolute necessity if she is ever going to learn to paint? For one or two days a week she will paint in a way that has a meaning and a purpose. At last! She can't wait

*Copy of El Greco's Christ Driving the Money Changers from the Temple*

*Copy of a Turner sunset*

to tell Noreen.

Is her investment of hope overwhelmingly naive? Certainly her new-fired enthusiasm is observed and noted by those around her. She has, after all, made an overnight transition from a reluctant, depressed, unmotivated student to one who strides around the place with a new purpose, and it worries those who know her well and care about her. One day she finds a note in her pigeon hole. Professor Coldstream wishes to see her again. Will she please drop by his room.

'So you're enjoying yourself at the National Gallery? I see you are still going two days a week.' He raises an eyebrow. 'At least.'

'Yes, of course. It's the best possible opportunity. It's what I want to do.'

'But you're neglecting your painting here. You're skipping classes.'

'I reject the style taught here and I'm learning much more from copying.'

'Listen, Rosa. Please hear me out. As your father's friend, I feel a responsibility for you. I've been watching your progress over the years. The thing is...it's fine to spend *some* time copying in the National Gallery as part of your art education, but I worry that it's getting out of hand. This is not the way to learn. You do know, don't you, that your passion for standing all day copying the same ancient painting will ruin you as a contemporary artist? And you do have talent. You do want to be a painter, don't you?'

Silence. This is not what Rosa expects to hear. Does no-one understand?

Rosa slowly gathers her things, gets up and walks away. *I decided that if knowing the techniques would ruin my artistic vision, then I didn't have much artistic vision.*

She ignores the advice of her father's friend. She ignores her tutors' heavy hints that she has spent enough time in the National Gallery and should return to the painting studios at the Slade. She ignores anyone who tells her she is old-fashioned and blind to the exciting possibilities of modern painting styles. Rosa's resolve is firm. Here, amongst the great painters admired so much by her father, she is completely at home, blissfully content to join the many other painters and students who, over the decades and centuries, have stood as she now stands, before the tradition of learning by copying went out of fashion. Among the ghosts of the great painters and the ghosts of their admirers, finally she is starting to understand and develop the techniques she has waited so many years to learn.

For Rosa the National Gallery is a place of joy and warmth and brilliance. She feels privilege and excitement as she wanders from room to room and stares up at the glorious paintings before properly starting her day. She collects her easel from a room at the back and sets it up in front of the Tintoretto she has chosen to copy. The feet of the easel exactly mark her possession of this space with tiny scratches and dents. Having unpacked her paints, her charcoal, her brushes, she works with great concentration to interpret and reproduce the painting in front of her: the turn of a head, the fold of fabric, the colour of the sky. Which colours were mixed to make that grey-blue? How was the atmosphere of warmth and vivacity created? It's not work, more a delight to look inquisitively and with love at a much admired painting with the challenge of unravelling the technique that produced its elements of composition, shape, line, texture and perspective. And the light. Always the light.

Working near and alongside her is a group of young restorers, learning their trade, learning, like her, to understand the building of layer upon layer so that they know the process and can repair any damage to old paintings. Their tutor is the same Dr Ruhemann who gave the three inspiring lectures at Camberwell on how to create a painting in the style of Rubens. He adopts Rosa and includes her in his group, encouraging them and gently offering advice when he does his rounds once a week. Rosa is there, concentrating, painting like mad, oblivious to anything outside the frame of the painting, and suddenly a very polite gentleman stops behind her and looks over her shoulder. 'Why don't you try that?' he says, mildly. 'You'll find it works.' And it does.

The Gallery can be nearly empty or busy with visitors and artists, some of whom stop to watch Rosa painting. She likes that. It reinforces her feeling of being a part of the place, of being part of the life of the gallery. Visitors who stop and watch over her shoulder don't distract her. Her confidence grows and with it her absolute certainty that here she has found the right way to learn to paint. This time in the Gallery is crucial and significant. Rosa's ambition, thwarted, dismissed and discouraged, blossoms here under the eyes of the men and women painted by Rembrandt and Titian and da Vinci. Rosa has come home. *It changed my life. My ambition was to paint the contemporary world with the same techniques as the great Renaissance painters.*

\* \* \*

Many years later, married to Alan Hopkins, and when her two children are at school, Rosa returns to the National Gallery to copy more paintings. *I copied Claude because I wanted to paint the beautiful blue skies. I copied an early Turner because I wanted to see how he did it. I copied a Titian because I wanted to see how he did it. A Francesco because I wanted to see how he did it. I copied a Rembrandt. I mean there were certain things that each painter did.*

# The Slade: life class
# 1953
# Age 20

On the very first day at the Slade, at the first gathering of all the new students in one of the halls, Rosa catches a glimpse of a man who makes her break off her conversation mid-sentence. She stares openly and rudely, thinking, *'That's the most handsome man I've ever seen in my entire life.'* Rosa's first, indelible impression of Alan Hopkins is a visual one.

So yes, she had already noticed him around the Slade. So, too, had the few other female students whose eyes followed him down corridors and gazed briefly, admiringly, perhaps longingly at him across studios when he flaunted his paintbrush with panache. Although he carried his sparkling charisma lightly, he knew he drew others to him. He was, perhaps, the brightest star in their firmament.

Rosa is one of several women in the Antiques Room, drawing a plaster hand and wrist, a cast of part of a Renaissance sculpture. She's been told to draw it with single clean black lines and no shadows. 'Bloody awful! A cartoon not a drawing,' she mutters to herself, hating the task. The other women in the room chatter as they draw but Rosa stays inside her bubble of solitude, the only noise the angry scrape and squeak of charcoal on her sheet of paper and her sighs of dissatisfaction. Alan, waiting for the life class in the room next door, has had his eye on this troubled young woman for some time but he's been biding his time, waiting for the perfect moment, because she is often absorbedly absent and unapproachable. Seeing her frowns of frustration, he decides to pounce.

'That's good,' he comments, striding across the room and briefly leaning over her shoulder, but she's canny and knows it's only an opening gambit because he's barely glanced at what she's done. His eyes are on her, not her drawing. It's not in her nature to play coy – she is far too open for such games – but she does carry the memory of being told she was the most beautiful girl at Camberwell so she doesn't shy away from the glances and advances of young men. She looks up. Seeing him close for the first time, she thinks this man is terribly handsome, and very sure of himself.

'Why don't you drop that and sneak into the life class?' he says, teasing, his eyes not leaving her face. 'You can draw real hands.'

'You may be allowed to draw real people and skip this boring stint in the Dead Room, but we mere women are not allowed in the life class until we've finished our punishment in here and our tutors are satisfied we can draw plaster people,' she replies. 'They segregate us, for heaven's sake, as if staring at a nude form will somehow provoke a hormonal explosion.'

He grins. 'There'll be quite a few hormonal explosions today. There's a beautiful young woman posing. More enticing than the usual weary souls they send us.'

He winks at Rosa and runs out, joining a scrum of young male students trying to get in the door. They're pushing and shoving, cracking jokes, peering over shoulders to catch a glimpse of the shapely figure sitting still and naked and unperturbed on the dais. Near her, a stove casts a red light across the floor while the smoke from dozens of cigarettes rises to form a blue cloud that has nowhere to go. Coke and tobacco dim the air, but the woman is still gloriously visible.

An hour later, Alan is back, brandishing a large sheet of parchment paper which he hands to Rosa. The lines of the drawing are strong and fluid, the portrait powerful and epic.

'It's bloomin' good,' she acknowledges. And it is. It's superb. This man is as brilliant as the grapevine says.

'Already sold it to the caretaker!' He laughs. 'The man was watching at the door, nosy beggar, and took one look at this when I came out and made me an offer. Sold!'

He's gone again and Rosa feels she's been caught up and whirled round until dizzy and dropped again. She turns back to the cast of the hard, lifeless hand and sighs.

The next day, he's back. Rosa is seated in the same room, drawing with the same stubborn precision and dissatisfaction, scowling at the curled fingers of the plaster hand because it needs shading to make it live on the paper. The damn thing's dead and stays dead.

'That's a good drawing,' he says, not bothering to conceal his grin, his hand on her shoulder. Something in his expression tells her that this is a game whose moves he often practises.

'No, it isn't. It isn't very good at all,' she replies, putting down her charcoal and watching his beautiful face. 'I can't do a good drawing without shadows.'

'No, you're right, it's bloody awful. I'm trying to chat you up. Will you come to the pictures with me?'

Rosa is tempted but decides not to concede quite so quickly. Let him wait.

'Certainly not,' she replies, trying to hide laughter that threatens to spoil her stern expression.

'Right,' he says, and marches to the other side of the room and goes through exactly the same routine with another girl who giggles and blushes and doesn't turn him down. Rosa hears every word of the repeated refrain and smiles. It's a game.

The following day, she's expecting him and is so excited she hasn't even started to sketch the horrible hand. Distraction, for Rosa, is rare indeed. She knows she's a willing accomplice in a cat and mouse game and that all his nonsense is a play for her attention and her attention alone. That she finds him entrancing, funny and charming is beyond doubt, but the other half of the equation also nicely adds up. He's a brilliant painter. Everyone says so. She couldn't spend time with anyone who isn't. What would they talk about? How would they respect each other? Anyone auditioning for the role of Rosa's soulmate had better be an artist at least of equal standing. Clive Branson's shadow falls across her, as it often does, a ghost painter who walks beside her in rooms which he too once occupied. *My daddy was a great big handsome funny bloke who did lovely paintings and he was such fun and made jokes.* He's a hard act to follow. Can this young man stand comparison?

'Now will you come to the pictures?' Alan asks, dropping down beside her and covering her hand with his.

He *is* brilliant, Rosa thinks. And agrees to go out with him. The ghost nods. *We fell in love and within two days I asked him to marry me.*

*I only stayed at the Slade for a year because I met my first husband… and I discovered we were being taught by the same people as we'd learnt from at Camberwell and then I thought this is stupid, this is hopeless.*

\* \* \*

Rosa and Alan become inseparable. Others watch and smile. If they were in a painting, they would be in sharp focus, very detailed, brightly lit, while the background of people and places would be faded and blurred.

Transpose them to another background, and it would be the same. Only the two central figures glow with energy and light.

'Listen,' Alan says, trying to sound grave and taking Rosa's hand as they wander along the banks of the Thames. 'There is something I need to tell you. Something you need to know about me.'

Both have their sketchbooks. Both have been sitting for hours pretending to draw fishermen working on some old boats tied up at the riverside, but neither has been concentrating, and Alan keeps making Rosa laugh by being outrageous and imitating people they know and impersonating their tutors. To perfection. Their hands stray to one another instead of to charcoal and paper.

'Seriously, Rosa,' Alan continues, not looking serious, 'I need to tell you something.' He is trying to match his words with an earnest face, but it's hopeless. He doesn't have a gloomy bone in his body. He is electric and he dazzles. 'Look, listen. I was once admitted to Shenley Hospital, when I was a teenager.'

Rosa looks up. 'The mental hospital?'

'Yes. There's something wrong with my head and every five years I go off the rails.' The way he tells it, it sounds like a bit of a joke. Certainly nothing to worry about.

'What happened? What was it like?'

'Oh…they put me in this ghastly nightdress and I decided to run away and I ran all the way across the hospital grounds and through fields with all the doctors and nurses chasing me, but I was much the fastest runner. It was so funny!'

'Did they catch you?'

'No chance.'

The story, told with panache, makes firm a resolve that Rosa has been harbouring since she first encountered this good looking, entertaining young man. There is a moment's silence while she makes her decision. 'Will you marry me?' she asks. A while back, she grew fond of a different young man who told her, quite late in the relationship, that he'd been engaged to someone else for four years. It was then that she resolved to propose marriage to any likely candidate within ten days of meeting him. And so she has.

Is Alan taken aback at this request from a woman? Isn't he the one who's supposed to propose? He fully intends to.

'No, Rosa, because I'll ruin your life.' He doesn't sound very convinced about the harm he will inflict, and scowls and frowns and pulls dreadful faces which only make Rosa laugh more.

'It will take more than you to ruin my life,' she says, shoving him. He can't be serious.

'In that case, I'd love to.' He shoves her back and then their arms are round each other's waists and Rosa's head is on Alan's shoulder.

'Well, I've told you,' he says.

'You have. And being a painter doesn't make any of us normal,' Rosa replies. To have this brilliant man here at her side is both miraculous and utterly right. 'Do you know, Alan, I've had a few men who've proposed to me... Listen, one banker said that when we got married, I could stop painting and I'd be awfully good at making curtains for the kitchen. Honestly, he thought we'd be really happy. And I thought, you might be really happy, but I'd be bored stiff.'

'I want to marry a painter,' Alan replies.

And so it is done.

*As far as I was concerned, being a painter didn't make one normal at all. And anyway, what about me? I come from an aristocratic family, I'm the daughter of revolutionaries who joined the Communist Party, and my best friend ran wild in a gang smashing light bulbs, so I'll never fit in.*

She is not alarmed about Alan's past. Not even slightly worried. If there are warning bells, she doesn't hear them.

# 9 THE WIFE AND ARTIST

## 1954
## Age 21

They marry within weeks. Alan continues studying at the Slade while Rosa leaves, already planning to have children. Not that leaving is a penance. She walks out of the place with bounding steps and a new freedom. With neither of them much bothered about their surroundings, they rent a small flat in Camden Square which is all they can afford. As long as they have a space that provides good light for painting – and it does – they have all they need. The two young artists settle right in with their easels, their paints, and their easy love for one another. It's a glad, giddy, carefree time. A time of enormous creativity.

But it's not long before Rosa is in despair. The visions, which have accompanied her through childhood, adolescence and into marriage, have stopped. Where once she stepped between her parallel worlds of the here and now and the imagination, now there is only ordinary everyday reality.

'The visions! They've gone.' Rosa is hunched on the sofa, lost and bewildered. Noreen can see that she has shed tears. She's dropped in briefly to check up on her daughter, having noticed a growing unhappiness despite her pregnancy that, so far, is going to plan after a previous miscarriage.

'It's because you're pregnant,' Noreen tells her.

'But I can't paint without the visions. You know that. From that first time when I saw the tiger with the flaming eyes in the rhododendron bushes at school, and no-one else could see it, they've always been there, wherever I go.'

'I know, darling. But they'll come back.'

'Part of me is missing.' Rosa is distraught.

'It's temporary. They'll return. Twenty-four hours after you give birth, you'll have your visions back.'

'How do you know?'

'Because when I was pregnant with you, I couldn't think straight and I couldn't write. I used to sit at my typewriter for hours and couldn't find any clarity. Nothing made sense. My brain was fog. Then twenty-four hours after you were born, my ability to think clearly came back, like a part of my brain had fallen out and found its way back in.'

'But aren't writing and painting different? You don't have visions.'

'I don't think they're different. We're both creative people and it's that part of the mind that shuts down, maybe to protect us and stop us thinking all the time and getting too tired. Our bodies are telling us to go into a kind of hibernation until we give birth. Perhaps it's to protect the unborn child.'

'But the visions are so important, Mummy. Like my own private films. I know they aren't real, but they're real to me, and they're my inspiration.'

'I know. I know.' Noreen has heard all this before, but she's here to reassure her daughter so listens again with a quiet patience.

'They are such a joy! Such fun!'

'Rosa, listen to me, the visions have faded only because you're pregnant. They'll come back.' Noreen's sympathy is wearing just a bit thin.

Rosa looks up, breathes more slowly. Noreen is always right.

'I hope you're right. Just imagine in the olden days when women got pregnant about fifteen times? And other people thought they were really stupid. Poor things. Their imaginations would have shut down completely every time. How on earth did they cope?'

'Most weren't painters or writers,' Noreen replies, pragmatic as ever. 'Their lives consisted of looking after their husbands and their children, their domestic duties relentless and exhausting. Terrible to go through so many pregnancies though, and to know that some of the babies wouldn't survive long into childhood. To say nothing of the mothers' poor health.'

'How awful not to know imagination and passion,' Rosa says, more to herself than to Noreen.

'It's not so different now. In some areas,' Noreen continues, following her own train of thought. 'There are women with seven or eight children living in terrible poverty. A big family crammed into two or three rooms with no privacy or space to call their own. Constant noise and upheaval. I see the conditions when I visit them.'

'I know you do. I shouldn't complain.'

'You will survive and survive with your visions back. Be patient, Rosa. You need to wait another six months. And then you'll have a lot more to think about than visions, I promise you!'

Rosa smiles, but at the moment the baby, though longed for, does not have much reality. 'Maybe it's hormones,' she says.

'Could be.'

'Maybe the change in hormones makes us concentrate on the practical. The essential. Hormones make us focus on the survival of our babies and close down our imaginations.'

'It's a convincing theory though I know of no evidence one way or the other.'

'Anyway life's become very dull with no surprises waiting for me. I feel sorry for people who don't see them.'

'But if they've never seen them, they don't know what they're missing.' Noreen gets up to take her leave. She has work to do. Her daughter will get through her pregnancy without her visions!

'Thank you,' Rosa says as she kisses Noreen at the door. 'Sorry to complain.'

'I understand.'

And Noreen is off, and along the road. Walking very fast, as she does. Rosa notices the ladder in one of her stockings.

Over the following four years, Rosa becomes pregnant three times, and suffers two miscarriages. Each time, while she is carrying the baby, the same thing happens. The visions stop as suddenly as if someone has thrown a switch. Always it's a blow. Without them, she feels her imagination veiled and in darkness. Without them, her world closes down into something drab and mundane. Someone has turned down the brightness and the contrast. The picture is flat and monochrome. She moves through grey. But after each miscarriage, and after each birth, the visions return. The two halves, Rosa's real and imagined worlds, merge again. By the time she is pregnant for the fourth time, with the son she will carry to term, she manages not to panic. She trusts that twenty-four hours after the birth, a siamese cat with yellow eyes or a dragon with purple wings will climb onto her hospital bed to nestle there alongside her newborn baby. And she will smile her welcome. Noreen is right. She usually is.

# Horses
## 1955
## Age 22

Peggy is born. Rosa's visions return. She embraces her tiny new daughter, and when she pushes the pram, the cats and monkeys and birds of paradise spring from behind trees and dance along the pavement at her side, just as they should. In the park, creatures lie in the grass close to the other mothers and children who can't see them staring up at them with shining eyes. Life is rich and beautiful.

In the small flat in Camden Square, there is no discussion and no arguments about their adoption of fairly conventional gender roles. Alan continues at the Slade while Rosa stays at home with Peggy, and later with her son Michael. They accept the pragmatic way. What else is there to do? Alan is a brilliant artist and must continue his education and his career.

But Rosa is determined not to let mothering snuff out her creativity and puts in place a routine that prevents her lapsing into mental laziness. It's fairly punishing and requires stamina, but it ensures she remains engrossed and challenged. During the day, she puts away her easel and oil paints because tiny fingers might transfer poisonous pigment to tiny mouths. It's simply not safe to carry on painting. A friend of hers has a child who drank a bottle of turps and had to be rushed to the emergency department of the hospital. Fabric replaces paint, remnants of silk, velvet, lace and linens which she cuts into pieces and organises according to colour and texture. While her children crawl and play at her feet, or sleep away the hours, and later when they are old enough to amuse themselves in an adjoining room, she sits for long hours at her table in the window and creates magical scenes by layering and overlapping scraps of material, holding the pieces in place with her minute stitches. These collages carry echoes of her painting in the layering, and in the way she stitches in the broad shapes and background pieces first, then adds smaller pieces and finer detail, until she is stitching pinprick stars. They are intricate and beautiful and elaborate. It is slow, time-consuming work that requires immense concentration, but given that her children are still young, and she needs to earn her living, she accepts that this is what she does in the mornings. And it's not as if she's taken a completely new artistic turn. While at Camberwell, embroidery was her second subject, a choice very much influenced by the beautiful Chinese embroideries in her grandparents' home, Rise House, on the outskirts of Sevenoaks in a road known locally as Millionaires' Lane, where she stayed during her holidays as a child. Rosa was happy there with her grandmother teaching her how to sew and encouraging her to walk round the room with a book on her head so she would have good posture.

And like the layers of velvet and silk held together in the tapestries,

Rosa and Alan remain interconnected in so many ways. The marriage is a happy one. When the children are in bed, they talk about painting. And politics. These are the unbroken threads in the fabric of their lives.

* * *

'I'm coming too,' Rosa says one day when she finds Alan painting a placard with the words NO GERMAN ARMS. 'We've been through two world wars. The country is sickened by the very thought of another.'

'I'd rather you stayed here, Rosa. In your condition. From what I've heard, there's going to be a crush and it could get tense.'

'Exactly. I'm coming. I feel as strongly as you do. Mummy is coming too.'

'She's not pregnant.' Alan gives Rosa a piercing stare.

'I'll stay at the back,' Rosa bluffs, knowing it won't wash.

'Back or front. What difference does it make?'

'The demo is outside the House of Commons. All we're doing is waiting in line to lobby MPs, Alan. I read that the capitalist world is frightened of Europe turning communist!'

'Communism is a dirty word, Rosa,' Alan replies. 'You of all people know that.'

'War is dreadful. Daddy died fighting in Burma.'

Alan knows Rosa has added the full stop to the argument. Further persuasion will be futile. Rosa will be at his side no matter what he says. For her father, and for peace.

'There's absolutely no appetite for another war,' Alan says. 'I hope the protest will be peaceful and swift. We must get the message across to those in power. If it goes smoothly, we'll get into Parliament, say what we have to say, and leave again.'

They shrug on coats and hats. Noreen calls down that she'll follow later. They leave, Alan carrying his placard. It's a cold January night with the smell of fog hanging like sulphur all along the streets. The lamplight is hazily dim.

There's an orderly queue waiting in a line to be allowed inside the Houses of Parliament to lobby. Rosa's heart swells with pride that so many people care enough to turn out on a night like this. The police, on foot and on horseback, block the entrance, but hold their line, calm and still. At first the queue is patient. They wait. They shout their demands and hold up their placards, but with restraint. An hour passes, and the gates remain closed, and more come to join those in the line. Another hour. Word must have got out that the protesters are being denied access because hundreds more convene, and the newcomers don't stand in line but spill out onto the streets in a flowing, noisy demonstration. Rosa watches, not from the back, but away from the crowd's heart, and hears the moment when impatience gives way to something more dangerous.

'We don't want war!' It's a lone voice.

The words hang, then the slogan is repeated and echoes down the line of waiting protesters until hundreds of voices chime in angry unison.

Another shout goes up. 'Down with arms for Germany.'

That too swells until the chorus chant beats its wings in frantic rhythm, like a murder of crows above Westminster. There's a thrill in being part of a great surge of people with a united purpose and Rosa is carried along on the tide of massed, pent-up energy. When her attention occasionally wanders, it is to imagine Clive painting this scene, painting the righteous indignation and frustration, the anger and despair in the men's faces. Her daddy would have captured all of this with his own fervour and honesty – people ignored and diminished and denied a voice.

Then something breaks. Patience ends. Anger overflows. They've been kept standing in the cold for too long and feel the contempt with which they are being treated. Those who arrived early expected to be allowed inside the building fairly quickly, but now, after three hours, there's no sign of movement. The message that passes from man to man, woman to woman, is that the gates will not be opened and they will not be allowed to say what they have come to say. They have been thwarted.

A few men break away and run at the police who easily block their way, for now impassive.

'D'you want another bloody war?' One man yells at a policeman.

'You should be bloody ashamed of yourselves.'

'Get out of the way and let us in.'

'Move! Move!'

Their words are utterly ineffective. Why waste their breath? It's time for action. Some of the protesters run at the officers on foot, screaming curses and spitting ire. There's a scuffle, some pushing and shoving, but nothing rash. Then a few, unable to limit their fury to hurling insults, edge through the police boundary on the ground until they are up against the hot flanks of the horses. Something gives. Impatience boils over, and fists pound the horses' flesh. Protesters leap up to grab hold of reins and bits and bridles. The horses show the whites of their eyes and toss their magnificent heads. Threatened, they begin a slow, rhythmic dance, hooves tapping out a readiness to leap forwards. Their riders sit back and hold them steady.

Alan shakes his head. 'This won't help. This is not what was planned. It's asking for trouble.'

Rosa watches, spellbound and aghast. 'They're taking on the police!'

A mounted policeman raises a megaphone and the order comes over, brittle and loud and clear. 'Move on! Move on! Parliament is sitting. You are not allowed to assemble here. Anyone not queuing in an orderly line is asked to leave. Only a single line.'

The protesters boo and hiss.

'I repeat. Move away. Disperse.'

No-one budges.

'You have been warned.' The policeman with the megaphone repeats, louder. 'Move away or we will have to move you.'

'Oh no!' Rosa shouts, pulling on Alan's sleeve. 'Look!'

The red-faced men who are right up against the horses are aiming their boots at the animals' fetlocks, vicious and hard. The horses respond with a backwards dance, a sideways dance, trying to escape pain. The mounted police lean down to knock the men away, like buzzing flies from their horses' necks.

'There's blood on the horses' legs,' Rosa says in dismay. 'They're hurt. This has gone too far.'

'Let's go,' Alan says. 'Now. Before things turn really nasty.'

He grabs her hand and leads her away through the crowd.

A command is given and as one, the horses inch forwards towards the protesters. High-stepping, almost in slow motion, they move in a dance formation, metal shoes ringing brightly on the cobblestones. At first, the demonstrators stand their ground, some still aiming cruel blows at the horses' shins. But then they hesitate. They turn. They flee.

Only to re-form in much greater numbers near Leicester Square, surging towards Cambridge Circus. What began as a few hundred people waiting to lobby Parliament is now a mob of several thousand, angrier than when they started because no-one was willing to hear them. Alan and Rosa stay with the protest.

The horses are back. In the distance, a long line of mounted police, thirty or forty strong, clips its way closer and closer – formidable, threatening, powerful. They are massive, those horses, heads tossing, nostrils flared, prancing and dancing on the spot, contained only by the skill of the men on their backs. The massed horses, nudging flank to flank, are brought to a halt thirty yards from the demonstrators, facing them. The animals are restless now, snorting steamy breath in the cold air and pawing the road. The police sit immobile on their backs, controlling the horses with the merest movement of a wrist, the press of a thigh, waiting for the order. Then, as one, they are moving towards the crowd, bearing down on them. A few protesters stand firm until the last minute, but in the end, they all run. They scatter into doorways, flatten themselves against walls, race into side streets as the horses charge. Alan turns and runs, calling after Rosa, but he's caught in the terrified crowd and carried forwards. Rosa stays longer, longer than most, heart pounding, finding all of this hugely exciting and vivid and inspiring. At the last moment, she too peels away, arms held under her bump as she runs for safety.

When she bursts through the front door, Alan is already back at his easel, the first lines of a new sketch echoing the energy and the anger.

'My goodness, Rosa, you left it til the last minute!' he says, his face pale and his forehead creased in concern. 'I ran, and when I looked back you were still rooted to the spot. I couldn't turn back to get you because the crowd was pushing me forwards. Why didn't you run with me?'

'I stayed until it wasn't safe. I was entranced by the horses.'

Alan sighs his exasperation. 'You wouldn't have stood a chance! None of them stood a chance. The horses would have trampled the lot of you underfoot. Don't romanticise them.'

'I'm going to paint it!' Rosa calls. 'The horses charging. Those wonderful, courageous animals.' Throwing off her hat and coat, she reaches for her sketchbook, sees in her mind the finished composition, one of mass movement and mounted tension. 'You know I used to paint horses when I was at Springfield Grange School. They're magnificent.'

'I'm not too fond of them when they're charging at me.'

'I think it was terribly exciting.'

'Rosa, it was dangerous.'

'Well, we have to stand up for what we believe in. Others before us have.'

Alan shrugs, frowns, and turns back to his sketch.

Rosa paints with fervour. She paints as if horse flesh is transparent, the great bones and sinews and cartilage as visible as scaffolding. Only then, with the flesh added, will a pose or a movement convince.

* * *

At the police station, where Rosa has brought her finished work to show the men, they trip over one another's sentences to praise her portrayal of the majesty of the animals.

'Was you demonstrating or admiring the horses?' one of the men jokes.

'Both,' Rosa replies.

Well, they're a good likeness.'

'Did you know that two of the horses needed treatment after they were kicked so viciously?' A man with a quiet voice has joined the group and is leaning over Rosa, examining her work.

'How awful. I'm sorry.'

'You're very talented.' This man in uniform has a quiet dignity. Rosa wonders if he is in charge here. 'Would you like to draw more of our horses?'

'Yes! Of course I'd love to,' Rosa replies, wondering if he's going to reveal the date of the next demonstration.

'I can give you permission to spend time in the police stables in Kentish Town, if you like. You can go in whenever you want and draw the horses. There are some beauties.'

'I'd love to,' Rosa repeats, not believing her luck.

'Go when you want. I'll let them know. And come back and show me what you've done.'

Rosa is elated. She has a new purpose. Off she goes, day after day, sketchpad and pencils and charcoal in her bag, and she stands for hours on end in the yard while the stable lads heave straw in and out of the boxes with pitchforks, and polish the tack. Horses are led out and saddled and bridled. Horses are exercised in a sand-filled ring. Horses are ridden in and out of the yard.

'Why are you drawing the horses?' a groom asks in passing.

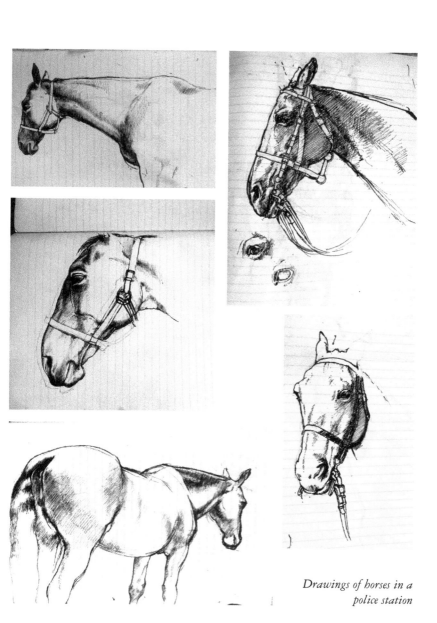

*Drawings of horses in a
police station*

'Oh...I'm going to do a painting of the coronation,' she lies. 'I'm learning my trade. Learning to draw the animals properly,' she says to herself, as if the truth needs to be out.

Every time she arrives in the stables, the Union Jack on the post by the gates is raised by the duty policeman.

'Why does the flag go up when I arrive?' she asks him.

'Rules,' comes the reply. 'It's the signal to all the men that there's a lady on the premises so they must watch their language.'


## The Highgate House
## 1955
## Age 22 to 26

The flat in Camden Square is intimate for two newlyweds. It's a good enough space for two young artists. For two parents who paint, and a baby, it is crammed and crowded.

'How about I buy a house? Would you two like it if we shared a house?' Noreen asks when visiting one cross day when Alan has twice tripped over the pram jammed in the hall, and Rosa has run out of places to store her embroidery collages. 'Supposing we all move to a big house where there's plenty of room for all of us? I can give you a bit of help with Peggy, but we'll still live our separate lives. What do you think?' She pauses. 'I've started looking, on and off.'

'That would be wonderful, Mummy. Wouldn't it, Alan?'

'Brilliant, Noreen. That's very generous of you. Do you need help with the search?'

'No. I can manage that, thank you. But I won't agree anything until we've all approved of it.'

It's a welcome idea. A timely idea. A solution to a growing problem and a growing family because Rosa hopes there will be more babies.

And so Noreen looks in earnest, turning down a first property as unsuitable, but quickly finding a second with potential.

'I think I may have found the right place,' she says, bursting in on them one day.

Alan puts down his paintbrush. Peggy wobbles to her grandmother.

'Where is this one?' Rosa asks.

'Highgate. At the top of a hill. The road climbs up from Archway Road. It's very pleasant.'

'Is it big enough for all of us? And our easels?' Alan asks, a broad smile lighting his face. 'We're a messy crew. And we spill a lot of paint.'

'I know. And yes, it will split easily into two separate spaces. At the moment it's a huge family house with six bedrooms over three storeys, and a basement. More than enough room.'

'I think it could only work if we had the ground floor. Would you mind, Mummy? So much paraphernalia and the pram and lugging that heavy Peggy about...'

'That's what I've already decided. I'll take the first floor. I can convert the biggest bedroom at the front into a sitting room and workroom. I can turn a smaller bedroom into a kitchen and there are still enough bedrooms for us all. You can have the whole of the lower floor with...'

'A studio?'

'...a big north-facing room for you to paint in. And there's a huge basement for storage. And a sloping garden for children to play in.'

Noreen has thought it all through before offering her plan. Rosa's face lights up. Alan grabs Peggy and throws her in the air.

'It will work wonderfully well, Mummy! All of us living together under one roof. Daddy would have been so happy.'

'I know he would, darling.'

'So what's the time scale?' Alan asks. 'How long before we all pack up?' He's still tossing his little girl in the air and grinning at her squeals of laughter, a restless fireball of energy.

'I've put in an offer which I hope can be finalised fairly quickly, but you need to go and look first. I insist on your approval. The house is empty so we shouldn't have to wait too long. If you like it, and they accept my offer, I'll need to get the rooms on the first floor converted quickly so that I can start working as soon as I move in. I think we're talking about a few months.'

When Noreen leaves, and Peggy is asleep, Alan and Rosa sit with mugs of tea, excitedly pondering the transition ahead.

'Why do you think she's doing this?' Alan asks.

'So that we can all be together, of course. She's very practical and she's also very helpful, Alan.'

Alan waits a moment, weighing his words. 'You know, I've always wondered if Noreen used to put her work before her daughter...no, hear me out, Rosa...I mean the way she sent you away all the time. Apart from those few years when you were small, you didn't live with your mother again until you were sixteen. You were at boarding school from six to sixteen.'

'There was a war on. Mummy was working as an air raid warden. She told me she wanted to make sure I didn't see bombs falling. She was protecting me, not neglecting me. She said we all had to be stoic and not complain.'

'But you saw so little of her, even in the holidays.'

'She had her reasons. And not just the war. She told me once that there was a psychological theory around the time of my birth that mothers are the worst people to bring up their children and that it's best left to others.'

'Sounds to me like a leftover from her privileged background. Let the nannies look after the kids while the ladies go to lunches and parties. Or was it an excuse she plucked at to justify her always working instead of spending time with her daughter?'

'That's nonsense! I'm proud of the work she did in the war. And that she's committed to the Communist Party and helping those less advantaged. She works very hard, Alan. She's writing pamphlets for the Labour Research Journal.'

Alan knows the lines by heart. 'Let me just say this...and I'm not wanting to cause offence or anything...but looking in from outside, one wonders if she might have been freer to concentrate on her work if she'd not been encumbered with a child.'

'She wasn't *encumbered*. She always found a way.'

'She risked imprisonment when you were just a baby, Rosa. Explain that to me. Even her communist friends were shocked. She volunteered to take documents to India knowing that if she were caught, she'd be arrested. It was a dangerous thing to do. She was putting her life at risk.'

'But she took great care, and planned it all meticulously. That was why she sent me to Dora Russell's school...'

'At the age of two, was it?'

'Let me finish...she went on a cruise ship and bought the most expensive clothes she'd ever had in her life so she'd fit in with the other wealthy passengers. With her background, it was easy for her to pretend to be a lady on a glamorous cruising holiday so she made sure the danger was minimal. Before she left, she had a suitcase made with a false bottom where she hid the documents. In India, she went to meet the revolutionaries during the day, and in the evenings she went to grand receptions and dinners. She even danced with the head of police in a ballroom in Bombay, and he told her he had a suspicion that there was a spy they hadn't yet caught! I think it's wonderful.'

'It was dangerous, Rosa...but I bow to her sang-froid!'

'She was brilliant.'

'Well, I have to admire her courage.'

'I know! Then, after she came back...it was some time later...they needed someone to cross the channel, go to Russia to collect documents, then meet revolutionaries all over Europe, so she volunteered again. This time she didn't have a suitcase. She wore a corset with the documents stuffed inside. One day she went to meet some revolutionaries up in the mountains and of course they asked to see the documents, and she said, 'Well, first I'll just have to go into another room!'

Alan roars with laughter. He can talk to Rosa about anything and everything, without anger, without either of them feeling threatened. He's still trying to track and understand the influences that played on this strong young woman before she became his wife.

'Did you never feel that Noreen...and Clive too...put their work before you?'

'Never! I was away at boarding school. And the point is, you see, I never felt they didn't care about me. Of course they cared about me, but they had tremendous ideals and aims. My contribution was not to complain. And they always told me how lovely I was and how much they loved me. They were wonderful people. Brilliant, lovely people.'

'It's generous of you to see them that way.'

'It's not generous at all! I was very lucky to have them as my parents. I'm still lucky to have Noreen. She's just offered us a home, Alan!'

Alan sees the truth shining in Rosa's eyes. This is what she believes, and maybe it *is* the truth. He will probably never know.

'Another thing, Alan...' Rosa is determined to make her point. She won't have her parents coloured with the slightest doubt. 'You know Noreen learned to fly? Well, she *adored* flying and flew everywhere for fun. When the war started, she talked to Clive about joining the war officially as a pilot.'

'Good God. Did she fly in the war?'

'No, no! Daddy said to her, "Don't. Rosa will be an orphan."' So she didn't, and became an air raid warden instead. So you see she did put me first.'

'Even so…it took your father to dissuade her from flying planes during the war!'

'And listen…' Rosa continues, ignoring the criticism. 'Do you know how she showed her love and concern for me when I was very young and she went out to meetings?

'Tell me.'

'She used to sit there and knit me a cardigan! Honestly, she took a very active part in Communist Party meetings while clicking away with her needles. Now that shows you what kind of a mother she was. And still is.'

Alan hides his amusement and wonders, not for the first time, if Rosa is looking at the past through rose-tinted spectacles. One mustn't shatter the story one tells oneself. Even so, a cardigan in a mother's hands instead of her child at her side. Does Rosa never question her mother's motives? Are her actions always to be explained away? And this new move, is it in some way for Noreen's convenience or for her daughter's? He decides not to raise that particularly thorny question. Either way, it suits him fine because Noreen will be around to give Rosa a bit more time to herself, when she's not working for the Communist Party. And he knows Rosa will be overjoyed with this late reunion with the mother she so rarely saw when she was a child.

And so it is. The Highgate house hums with the busy, purposeful life of three generations. Michael is born, and there's a free flow of traffic up and down the stairs, the children running up to be occupied by their grandmother for an hour before bedtime every evening, making things or drawing or listening to Noreen read. She likes the activities to be structured, not an excited free-for-all. The rules are strict and non-negotiable. Noreen's day is for work. The family downstairs can set their clocks by her rigid routine. *You knew what time it was by the time the typewriter started going and she would write two thousand words a day and she said if you're going to be a real writer you've got to write two thousand words a day and you actually edited it later. And that's what she did.* When not writing, Noreen attends meetings, and her communist friends call round for long, animated discussions which echo down through the floorboards. *My mother had a whole lot of friends who were revolutionary types. She said to me one day, 'We have a rule. We never discuss our health. We talk politics. We talk about the world. We never discuss our health.'*

Down below, Alan paints with a prolific, increasingly manic energy, though neither Rosa nor Noreen spot the early warning signs. His style, based on what was taught at the Slade, is one Rosa absolutely rejects for herself, but admires in his paintings. She is sure that he is a brilliant artist – after all, there is no way she could live with a painter whose work she doesn't admire and respect. While Alan works at his easel, she sits with stoic patience at her table in the living room window, embroidering fabric collages to sell to contribute to their income. In the adjoining room, the little ones play, the big cupboard doors wide open spilling toys and the railway set all over the floor. They know not to interrupt their mother and are content to amuse themselves. In the afternoons, Rosa takes them to the park and sits on a bench, smugly drawing the other bored, harassed mothers who don't go home to spend their evenings painting what they have sketched. You never hear Rosa complain that she has too much to do.

Between the age of twenty and thirty, Rosa is on a fast merry-go-round that never stops and always plays the same tunes. Her day is divided up with clinical precision, the mornings for embroidery, the afternoons for going to the park and sketching, the evenings, once the children are in bed, for painting. Her energy is formidable, but so is Alan's who is painting round the clock, increasingly oblivious of those around him. Rosa has to remind him to stop to eat. To change his clothes. To go to bed. The domestic agenda is Rosa's alone, but she allocates just one day a week for the boring chores. Her blitz of the rooms starts early, followed by the mountain of washing which is hung up to dry. As if this isn't enough, she develops a longing to play the piano. Like Noreen, perhaps. A friend, Jane Corbett, comes to the house to teach her, without charge, and she practises when the children are in bed. The fairground waltz plays on and on. For a while, no-one notices that the tunes become faster and the notes clashing and discordant.

From time to time, Alan's brother, Stuart, calls round to apply some pressure. From the moment he walks in the door, and takes in the organised chaos of painting and sewing and playing, his expression sours in disapproval. It's all so dreadfully bohemian.

'Look, Alan, isn't it time to stop messing about with oil paint and get yourself a proper job? You've got a family to support.'

It's his familiar opening gambit. Rosa and Alan expect it and exchange a resigned glance.

'I'm doing a proper job,' Alan always replies evenly.

'Have you any idea what I'm earning as an engineer?'

Alan doesn't deign to reply.

'Look, Alan, this is a stupid waste of your life. Give it up. Take some responsibility for your growing family.'

'We don't seem to be suffering.'

'Because you're supported by your mother-in-law.'

'Wrong,' Alan replies. 'We sell our work and live on the earnings.'

'Ah...but this house...'

'The situation is convenient for all of us, Stuart, as well you know.'

Stuart ploughs on. 'Look, we've just taken on an artistic chap like you in our firm. He's very useful. When we moved offices, he was really creative in the way he reorganised everything.'

'I'd love to reorganise an office...creatively,' Alan replies, his voice dripping with sarcasm. 'But meanwhile, if you don't mind, I'll just carry on painting.'

The lecture continues, as it always does, but eventually Stuart runs out of righteous indignation with no ground gained.

'Of course,' Rosa says, after he leaves and Alan shows the disappointment and upset he has hidden while in his brother's company

*War and Peace. Embroidered collage*

because some acknowledgement of his talent would be preferable to outright dismissal and rejection. 'Stuart is quite right. Poor Michelangelo, he got it entirely wrong. Instead of messing about on that ceiling, he should have got a proper job organising everyone's things in an office.'

The two of them collapse in howls of laughter. They are young and in love with art and each other. They are not easily put down.

*We all got on terribly well. Mummy wrote all her books at the kitchen table next to the window where she was high enough up to see Alexandra Palace. We worked downstairs in our studio. We were so happy when the children were born, me at work at the table doing drawings and embroidered pictures. Mummy said she only heard peels of laughter from downstairs.*

\* \* \*

The domestic harmony lasts five years when, jarred and unbalanced, it begins its slide into tension, fear, danger and disintegration. Although Alan told Rosa before they married about his mental illness, he did so in such a throwaway, funny manner that she heard only the comedy and not the truth – that he runs in predictable five year cycles which end when his charismatic, creative self unravels and descends into periods of terrifying insanity. *He was wonderful for five years, absolutely wonderful, handsome, joyful, funny, brilliant. But he was a real schizophrenic. He had two people in him. One of them was very handsome, a brilliant painter, very kind, very funny and absolutely gorgeous and we were gloriously happy for five years. Then he went mad. When he finally started to switch, he walked into his studio and smashed his easel.*

The Highgate house bears witness to the first five years of a sparkling marriage between gifted young artists and the birth of a second child. It sees the fallout from the first fault lines scored in a schizophrenic's mind, and afterwards, the full-blown, surreal extravaganza of his destructive madness. It contains the violence that bounces around the rooms on the ground floor and holds the breath-held anxiety of the mother upstairs who listens but does not interfere unless asked. It protects two small children from the ravings of an unhinged father and watches over the eventual parting of their ways. It shelters Rosa when her husband becomes too dangerous to keep at her side.

Later, it provides a base for two strong women who adjust to living without husbands. It holds their writing and their art.

But we are getting too far ahead in this story. We need to backtrack.


## Madness
## 1959 – 1960
## Age 26 and 27

*We were gloriously, happily married for about five years.*

The light is good today, bright enough to manage without the lamp. There is no wind so the clouds aren't skidding across the sun, creating an ongoing and frustrating alternation of blinding light and deep shade. It's hard to sew in those conditions. She is in her usual place, chair drawn up to the table by the window, her scraps of fabric, beads, needles and embroidery cottons spread out in front of her. She's working on an intricate collage of peacocks against a black sky of pinprick stars. It's painstaking work.

Today, in the next room Michael is playing with his trains on a wooden track spread over the floor and Peggy is sitting in her favourite corner reading out loud, their voices reaching her as a murmur through the open door, a peaceful hum that means she should be able to concentrate on the exact positioning of the tiny stitches needed to create the stars in the velvet sky. Today, though, Rosa is troubled and unable to lose herself in her fabulous design. Her face is clouded, her brow furrowed. Alan is not himself. He hasn't been himself for some time, though she has been slow to acknowledge the change. Her handsome husband, an endlessly flowing fountain of fun and energy and outings, has become a stranger. At first, the incremental shifts into a different persona were almost too small and infrequent to concern her, just passing clouds in an otherwise sunny sky, but the periods of harmony have grown shorter and are interrupted more often by bursts of temper and distress. She doesn't recognise this man of sullen moods and sudden outbursts. He rants and raves about visions that plague his imagination and that only he can see. His energy was always ferocious but now it's manic and confused, channeled into dark emotional seams that Rosa cannot access. During these outbursts, and recalling what he told her on a riverbank long ago, Rosa wonders if he is tipping towards madness. She brushes the thought away. Five years ago she was drawn to his exuberance and has been carried along in its effervescence ever since. His paintings are phenomenally alive. He'll tell her soon what is haunting him. Does she believe her own reassurances? She completes another minuscule star and sighs. She hates to be on guard like this, hates her concentration to be broken.

Days pass. The atmosphere in the Highgate house grows more electric and strained. Rosa and the children are on edge. Peggy bursts into unexplained tears, and Michael makes himself scarce. They walk on eggshells and hold their breath in case they disturb Alan's demons. It takes so little. Alan is still sometimes the man they know – funny and brilliant and charming – and Rosa hopes the crisis has passed. But the sudden mood switches come more often. She lives with a Jekyll and Hyde of a husband who disturbs and frightens her. One evening when she is painting in the studio, Alan bursts in, walks over to his easel and smashes it to pieces with his fists, his rage out of control and unstoppable. Rosa walks out and listens at the door, frozen, until silence tells her his anger has burnt itself out. She can hear him clearing up the mess. Rosa endures, knowing the time will come when something will give. One way or the other. Meanwhile it's a tightrope of a life with him.

Another day and Rosa is on red alert. Her embroidery is in her hands, and she wills herself to get on, to stop wasting time, but the air in the house crackles with tension and the silence is loud. She hears his heavy footsteps before he bursts through the door, pushing it so hard that it slams against the wall. She steels herself. Alan rushes at her, arms raised, eyes seeing what she does not. Curses and accusations that make no sense spill from his lips. Rosa drops her sewing and recoils. Fast to react because she is primed, she puts her hands up to protect her face but the blows rain down, hard and fast and painful. Too big and strong to push away, she kicks at the legs pressing on hers and cries out. Peggy comes running through.

'Mummy, why is Daddy hitting you?' she asks, her eyes wide with fear.

Alan spins round to face the new foe and raises a hand to his daughter. Rosa is on her feet, pushing hard, using every ounce of strength to knock him out of reach of the small child. His arms flail at nothing. Rosa faces him as he rants on. Standing right beside him, she shouts in his face, 'You touch that child and I'll kill you.'

He spins round and runs from the room, calling out to his demons.

'Coward,' Rosa mutters, drawing Peggy to her and comforting the trembling child. Michael has watched it all from a safe distance, holding on to the door jamb. Now he too runs for reassurance. Stunned and shocked, Rosa holds down her own fear while she reassures her children that they are safe, that their daddy is unwell and that he will be going away very soon. If she were outside looking in, she would want to paint the tableau of a mother wrapped around her children, the three figures rounded and merged into a single statue of love and protection.

Rosa is waiting for the right moment to act and she knows it has to come very soon, but after five years married to a man you adore, it is very hard to take the final irrevocable step. Alan has taken to roaming the house and garden, then pacing the streets, unable to settle for five minutes to paint. He asks an exasperated, worried Rosa to come for a walk with him on Hampstead Heath. She puts down her embroidery, asks Noreen to keep an eye on the children, and puts on her coat. Alan is pacing the hall, his eyes fixed on something visible to him alone. On the Heath, they walk fast, Alan talking about heaven knows what. The talking gets louder and more insistent until he is shouting wildly at the trees and the sky. People stare. Rosa puts a hand on his arm and forces him to stop.

'What is it?' she asks, frightened but determined. 'What's the matter, Alan? This can't go on.'

'I'm going to be crucified for the sins of the world because my birthday is the same day as the queen's and her birthday is the same as Adam and Eve's,' he replies, as if it's perfectly obvious that this is the problem. A massive, insoluble problem.

'That's mad!' Rosa says, not hearing the word until it is out.

He is still sane enough to understand.

'If you send me to a doctor, I'll kill myself and it will be your fault,' he tells her.

Rosa steers him round, heading for home and knowing she is taking this brilliant man to a necessary end to his freedom. There is no other option but to hold herself together and do what she has to do.

'The only way to be free is to kill yourself and the only way to kill yourself is to get everyone who loves you to hate you,' he tells her, as they walk back into the house.

Alan is admitted to hospital and Rosa visits him, clinging to a glimmer of hope that he will heal. With electric shock treatment, he seems better, calmer, more lucid, and is allowed home for the day. Then regularly. Then for overnight stays. At first, to protect them, Rosa takes the children to a friend before he arrives because she fears another outburst, but as time passes and there are no incidents, she decides the children can stay at home and be with their father. The mood is always strained and they sense all is not right. They are wary. They tread carefully. Two small observers watch from doors, listen at keyholes and play quietly within earshot.

'I'm going for a walk on the Heath,' Alan tells Rosa on one of his visits. 'Such a beautiful afternoon.' He sounds calm and matter of fact. He smiles at Rosa. 'I'll take Peggy. Let her roam.'

There's nothing to alarm Rosa, and Peggy seems content to be offered an outing. Off they go, father and daughter, while a mother watches from a window as they walk down the street, hand in hand. Michael carries on playing in the next room while Rosa works on her embroidery. An hour passes. Two. Three. Finally Alan returns and Peggy races past Rosa up to her room in floods of tears.

'What's the matter?' Rosa asks, panic rising. 'What have you done to upset Peggy?'

'I asked her if she would mind if I killed myself,' he tells her, as if it's the most natural thing in the world.

Alan has crossed a line that marks the point of no return. Once he is safely returned to the hostel attached to the hospital, Rosa visits him to tell him that their marriage is in effect over.

*It was awful. Awful. But I used it... When Alan went mad, I depended on my art to keep me sane... I don't regret marrying Alan. The other young men who proposed were normal and assumed I would give up painting and concentrate on being a wife and mother. In those days women didn't have careers. But I was determined to fulfil Daddy's dream so I married Alan.*

*I learned many things about madness. The paranoid thought they were God. The schizophrenics thought they were Jesus. The depressives wanted to die. The manic thought anything was possible. I came to the conclusion that people were mad when they couldn't cope with the real world.*

## Henry Hooper and the painting of oranges
## 1973
## Age 40

I was alone for six years. I said, 'Rosa, you'd better stop trying. You're no good at choosing husbands. You better get on and just paint.' So I wrote the whole thing off. I couldn't be bothered.

Henry Hooper comes up quietly behind Rosa at her easel, as he always does, and brushes a hand over her shoulder in passing. He knows to leave her alone when she's absorbed in her painting but he likes to glance in, observe her at work and admire her concentration. This time, however, he stops, hovers and frowns at what he sees.

'You're painting another picture of death.'

His interruption and his comment take her by surprise. She's been painting animal skulls for ages but has long since failed to ask herself why. At some point, she stepped onto a long conveyor belt of dark, satanic paintings, a reaction perhaps to Clive's death and Alan's violence, but now an exercise in technique that has slid into a habit. The current painting is of a deathly white goat's skull, its eye sockets looking blankly at grey mushrooms. All dust colours and shadows and sorrow.

'Not death, Henry. A still life. A composition...'

'It's a composition of grief and death. Why are you painting skulls?'

Rosa puts down her paintbrush and turns round. Perhaps he's right. Henry Hooper is so often right.

* * *

After the whirlwind that was Alan, this kind, capable, dependable man came into Rosa's life and offered her emotional and financial stability. He was the perfect husband and the ideal counterpoint for a woman who never wanted to be a conventional wife.

He told her, 'I want a dynamic career woman who is at home all the time so that I can phone her every day from the office.'

He is not joking. He really does want a wife who has her own interests and passions, and who does not lean on him for her happiness. Very early on he had told Rosa, 'Look, I don't have any ideas but I am a brilliant organiser. You tell me what you want and I'll organise it.'

'I'd love to paint the volcanoes of Java,' Rosa threw out almost as a joke, not imagining he'd take such an outrageous request seriously.

But he did.

'Right,' he told her not long afterwards. 'I've got it all organised. I've got six weeks off work owed me. We're going to Bali, Java, Sumatra, Malaysia and China. We're going by bus and train and boat and we're going to see all the monuments and do all the touristy things and we're going to end up at Raffles.'

And they did.

With Henry's protection and security came blessed release, and freedom. She doesn't have to worry about earning money because Henry provides for them. And her children are at school. Out comes Rosa's easel. With a great tide-rush of joy and relief, she reaches for her brushes and mixes her paints.

* * *

Now, she and Henry sit side by side on paint-splattered stools as the sun slides down the streaked sky and colours the easel and paints and brushes with a golden evening light. Even the skull and mushrooms are briefly relieved with some gold.

'You're happy with me, aren't you?' Henry asks.

'Goodness, you don't need to ask me. I have everything I want. I'm painting again.'

'But you're painting depressing skulls. Death.' His mouth twitches in a grin.

Rosa turns round to study what's on her easel. 'I hadn't thought about it like that. It's a still life, very much in the style of the Old Masters. I've explained it to you enough times.'

'Yes I know, but will you allow me to make a proposition?'

'Please do.'

'Why don't you paint fruit in shining silver bowls lit by candlelight and everyone will want to buy your paintings.'

'I don't care if people buy my paintings. I care about getting the technique right, Henry, you know that.'

'I do. I'm not suggesting you stop working on your technique. I'm saying how about painting arrangements of beautiful objects which people will love.' He pauses, before adding carefully, 'And incidentally want to buy.'

'We don't know that they will.'

'Will you humour me by testing my theory?' His arm hangs over her shoulder and she leans in to rest her head on his shoulder. Their marriage is solid and very fine.

'I'll finish the goat. Then I'll find the candles and light them,' Rosa replies. 'If that will please you.'

'It will please me greatly and I think it might please you as well.'

She hears the unspoken subtext. You don't live with a madman. Your life is safe. Your children are safe. I provide for you. I take care of you. You astonish and surprise me with your marvellous talent, your wonderful paintings, your never-ceasing passion for art. Our years are filled with loving companionship, travel and painting. But why haven't you turned the page in your art as you have in your life?

When she has finished the skull painting, and placed it propped up in the basement, Rosa goes to the market with an eye for beauty more than nourishment. On the stalls, she searches for colour and texture, her eye caught by apples with poison-red skin and oranges with lumpy, grainy peel. Grapes must be deep purple or palest green, crammed together in almost-ripe clumps. On her return, she tips the fruit from her shopping bag, polishes the apples with a tea towel until they gleam and rinses the grapes so that they are dewy with moisture. She places the fruit quickly, intuitively, to create gorgeous arrangements, on polished wood tables or on crisp white tablecloths. The candle is in a brass holder with a dish below which becomes an echo chamber of gold and silver light once the match is struck. She adds a bowl, a knife, a paper fan, old leather-clad books, a pearl necklace, a vase, a filigree butterfly brooch. In one arrangement, the burnished surface of a brass jug reflects all the other objects like a wondrously distorted mirror. In another, a portrait of Beethoven looks out from the pages of an old book at a violin lying on sheet music littered with green grapes. Candlelight embraces each miniature scene with honey-coloured warmth. Like a lamp-lit evening. Rosa places the candle, sometimes two candles, so that the flames flicker across the objects and penetrate deep into the shine of the wood.

Each painting is painstakingly detailed, the fruit so real you imagine picking it out of the frame and eating it. Rosa is prolific. Over the next few years, she completes twenty-five paintings, four foot by four foot, with Henry looking on in proud amusement and satisfaction. Although the arrangements vary, the paintings clearly belong together, the colours chosen from the warm spectrum of the palette, the mood opulent and rich. The animal skulls are laid to rest in bottom drawers.

## Dealers
## 1975
## Age 42

'Good evening, ma'am, I'm pleased to make your acquaintance.' He raises his voice a notch because so far his attempts to pin down the popular but elusive artist at the centre of this show have totally failed. She sidles away every time, nodding to someone else, making an excuse, wandering off to the other side of the room. Are her disappearing acts accidental? Rosa and Henry are at the opening of one of the later exhibitions of her candlelit paintings. They have sold well with galleries queueing up to exhibit them and Rosa giving nine one-woman shows so far. There's a crush of a crowd who stare and volubly admire, who want Rosa to themselves, who perhaps want to buy one of the gloriously calming paintings. With reluctance, she turns to the man who has been hovering at her side all evening, and whom she has been avoiding. From his shiny blue suit, his boring tie, his accent and his fixed smile, she knows that he is a dealer. She's never had a shred of interest in dealers, and manages to steer clear of them. There is no need for a middle man; she sells to friends and their friends as word gets round. But there's more to it than this, more than her professional indifference to the numbers game.

'I'm from Los Angeles, ma'am...'

He *is* a dealer. An American dealer, and she's not interested.

'These are wonderful paintings. Congratulations. Listen, I'm really interested in coming to some arrangement with you. It would be an honour. Tell me, how many paintings of oranges like these can you do in a year? I love the bright colour of the fruit and the warm candlelight. I

*Candlelit paintings*

can have paintings like this shipped over to America and sell them easily without you doing anything. I can sell fifty a year for you. A hundred! It will be a cinch. You'll get a good price. American collectors and folk who like art will definitely want to buy these gorgeous paintings, like something from the walls of an old English castle...'

It's as if a blind comes crashing down, extinguishing the candlelight that shines on fruit and brass jugs and jewellery.

'I'm not interested,' Rosa says, turning away, giving the man a stare that should put an end to any further bargaining. Her usually composed face is flushed. The dealer fails to see her distress, or badly misinterprets it as a first refusal or a tactic in a bidding war.

'Oh but wait...you've not even heard me out. My terms are very generous. I have an excellent reputation. Look, here's my card.' He produces a card but Rosa doesn't take it. 'With me behind you, you will be a painter who is in great demand in the States, as long as you carry on producing work like this...'

But Rosa is heading briskly for the exit, cutting short her time at her own exhibition. She links an arm through Henry's and steers him towards the door. Her husband sees the turmoil and upset in her face, and can sense a trembling fear. So unlike the Rosa he knows. This sensitive man waits until they are in a cab, heading home.

'What did that man say to upset you so much, my dear?'

'He frightened me,' she replies, telling him what he already knows.

'How?'

'He's a dealer.'

'Well...didn't you turn him away?'

'I'm sorry, Henry. I'm overreacting but I can't help it. I was friends with two artists who became famous in their forties, but dealers found them and got their claws into them and put them under huge pressure to produce more and more of the same kind of work. It became intolerable. They were caught on a never-ending treadmill.'

*Rosa and Henry on holiday*

*Henry Hooper posing as a homeless man. 'There were homeless people all over the parks after Maggie Thatcher came into power.'*

'What happened?'

'Each of them committed suicide.' Rosa sighs from the depths of her soul. How to assimilate the unnecessary, avoidable loss of two fine artists who were driven to despair?

'I'm sorry.'

'I'm not churning out paintings of oranges until my spirit is crushed and dead. I refuse to put myself in that position.'

'You don't have to,' Henry says.

Rosa does what she has done many times before. She changes tack, like a sailor on a boat heading towards inclement weather who adjusts the sails and alters course. At the market stalls, Rosa stops buying fruit, except to feed the family. At her easel, she paints miniature portraits, small perfect cameos of people she knows. 'I'm forty-two,' she tells herself. 'Goya took up portraiture at forty-two.' So she lets it be known in the neighbourhood and amongst friends that she wants to paint fifty portraits and the people of Highgate come flocking. These tiny portraits, exquisitely accurate in their detail, are of interest to no-one except those who sit for her. And, of course, Rosa.


## The candle goes out
## 1989
## Age 56

Rosa is in her forties and has been contentedly married for eighteen years when Henry is diagnosed with cancer of the kidneys. There is only one way to deal with this terrible body blow. Believing in her own psychic powers and her ability to influence events, she paints a picture of a single candle against a black background. The candle is Henry's life surrounded by his threatening death, but burning strongly and brightly, its flame not doused by the encroaching darkness. The light holds the dark at bay. Henry's surgery is successful. And so Rosa picks up her brush and carries on, painting 'life' again and again, represented in decanters of red wine and silver bowls lit by strong flames. These still lives radiate happiness. Rosa sells over two hundred and fifty candlelit paintings – without dealers – and has ten one-woman shows. These are good years – productive, prolific and very happy.

For now, death is banished. Rosa and Henry enjoy a long, joyful reprieve of ten more years, but then the candle splutters. Rosa is fifty-six when cancer returns. Henry's death from prostate cancer leaves her crushed with sorrow.

*I have learnt that when life is comfortable one paints comfortable pictures, but when life hits you badly, you come up with your best work. When Henry was dying, I created a painting of us meeting in heaven. It was eight foot by five foot and expressed exactly what I was feeling. It took nine months to complete. My daughter Peggy suggested I paint another, of the women left behind. People were kind and posed for me.*

*These two paintings transformed my life. Once again my career took off.*

# 10 THE PAINTER OF CHARITY STORYBOARDS

## A chance meeting on a cruise ship
## 1993
## Age 60

The death of Henry is huge and hard, a rock of a weight she carries in her heart. Rosa closes down into her cameo portraits, each one true and precise in its attention to detail. Her vision shrinks to eyes and lips, collars and necklaces, hats and brooches. It's easier than looking up and around at the bustling canvas of life that continues without her beloved husband.

Is it another instance of Rosa's intuition and claimed clairvoyance that takes her on a journey that will prove a release from her confining grief and diminutive paintings? Or just a lucky but random collision of souls on a ship bound for Norway? Rosa doesn't know it yet – how could she? – but the man who approaches her on the deck of the ship will swing open a door to twenty years of paintings that mark a new departure and that Rosa will come to consider her finest work.

She has taken herself on a cruise, wanting to shake off the sorrow that constrains and contains her in her work and in herself. It's time to raise her eyes to wider horizons, if she can, but without Henry, the world lacks colour and light. When the ship sails, she is thrown into the company of the other passengers, at meals and at organised activities, but she fails to engage. She's disappointed in her fellow travellers who are dull and self-important, tediously middle-class and conventional. Then, circling the deck one day, one of very few venturing outside because the wind is strong and the deck is slippery with salt spray, she spots another figure who wanders as she does and stops to stare over the rails at the sea gushing against the hull. He holds himself upright and seems absorbed in the movement of the boat through water. As their paced circles meet, he lifts his hat and smiles, and they fall into a conversation without an ending that they will pick up and put down and pick up again until the ship lands. And afterwards.

'Isn't it wonderful up here?' he says, perhaps not expecting a reply. 'I love the movement of a ship. I give myself over to it, and let the captain take us to our port. Not my responsibility.'

Now this is different from the usual opening gambits. This man is quietly confident and seems utterly content.

'You sound like a seasoned traveller,' Rosa replies. She looks up with her artist's eyes, noting the planes of a strong, craggy face and the warmth and wisdom in his eyes.

'I've had a lifetime of travel. I'm in my seventies, you know,' he tells Rosa.

'I'm in my sixties,' she replies. 'So what? The women in my family all live into their nineties so I've plenty of time yet.'

He smiles at her certainty. 'Well, I hope I can emulate them. But I can't do all that I once could.'

'And what did you once do?'

'I haven't stopped yet,' he chides. 'Nor will I while I can carry on and make a difference.'

It's Rosa's turn to smile. In recognition. 'Tell me what you do then.'

'Well…I started my working life as a commercial advertising man,' he tells her, taking his time to spin his tale while they continue their circumnavigation of the deck together, their eyes first on the horizon, then briefly on each other. 'But then I became a Quaker and had to ask myself if I could continue selling for mail order companies.'

'I can understand that,' she says with conviction, thinking it a poor calling for such a complete sort of a man. 'What did you decide?'

'I decided to work for the voluntary and humanitarian sector and use my experience there. I found myself a slot with the Oxford Committee for Famine Relief which you probably know as Oxfam. It's a world away from the traditional Lady Bountiful charities. Their remit is aid for refugees, and victims of war and natural disasters and famine. They desperately need our help, but they didn't have a clue about raising funds. That's what I did.'

Rosa smiles. An ideology spoken long ago by her parents blows in the wind and is carried in the damp spray from waves that splash against the ship's hull as it makes its slow progress through the sea.

'Fundraising for charities is fairly common, isn't it?' she asks.

'It is now. It wasn't when I started in the fifties,' he says. 'The charities were desperate for funding but didn't know how.'

What he doesn't admit to now, because this self-effacing man veers away from any hint of self-promotion, is that he is revered, admired and loved as the founding father of charity fundraising. This, Rosa will learn later, and respect him all the more for his reticence. It is Harold Sumption who first invented the fundraising advert containing shocking images and words which provoked readers into an immediate visceral response. Deliberately artless, almost crude, and always penned by him, they were effective in portraying depictions of need from which it was hard to turn away. Drawing on his skills and experience in commercial advertising, he knew what would work and what wouldn't work. He sought, and gained, a knee-jerk emotional reaction that led almost automatically to a donation. Initially, Harold made appeals for clothing and blankets, receiving an instant, massive response from the public. Later he asked for money, using the same techniques, and again the public gave. And gave. Harold Sumption was a pioneer in his field.

'Are you still working for Oxfam?' Rosa asks.

'Yes, and other charities. I've just been approached by Help the Aged. But enough of me. What about you?'

'I'm an automatic paintbrush,' Rosa replies. Is this the first throwaway remark she has managed since Henry died? She hears herself, and takes note.

'I confess I have asked around a bit, and I do know you are a painter. And I know that you favour the style of the Old Masters.'

'It's the only way to paint,' Rosa hurls back. 'I use the technique of the Renaissance artists to paint the modern world.' It's her dog-eared calling card. He can pick it up or leave it.

'I'd love to hear more. I'd like to see your work.'

'Well, you can,' Rosa says. 'Where do you live when you're not sailing to Norway?'

'Highgate.'

Rosa laughs. 'Really? I live in Highgate.'

Ah, another coincidence. Serendipity. He is almost a neighbour, and Harold interests Rosa, as she does him.

Back home, Rosa's curiosity leads her to ask friends if they know of him.

'Of course,' one acquaintance tells her. 'He's a very clever fundraiser and a wonderful speaker. I heard him talking about Oxfam and it moved an audience of hundreds to tears. He painted such a vivid, upsetting picture of people terribly in need. If Harold Sumption speaks, you know what the charitable world is really about. He can sell a cause, but he never sells himself. A sincere, unassuming but brilliant man. Why don't I invite you both to dinner?'

And so they meet again; they would have done without the dinner invitation. Rosa and Harold carry on their conversation and their friendship.

## Harold Sumption makes two propositions
## 1997
## Age 64

Perhaps inevitably, Harold Sumption asks Rosa to marry him. Ever-practical and with an eye on the future, Rosa says, *I refused because I would lose my pension. He was twenty years older than me and had already had three heart attacks so I would have been a fool to marry him, but I was very fond of him and we became a couple.*

* * *

It's an autumn evening in the Highgate house. Harold has been comfortably installed for months, the charity worker and the painter both content and purposeful, two like-minded people busy with their separate passions.

The two of them are sitting over a candlelit meal that echoes the paintings on the dining room wall. Harold has been waiting for the right moment and approaches his tricky topic like someone walking on eggshells.

'Rosa, you know all about my charity work...' he begins.

Rosa looks up. 'Of course I do! You told me on board that ship! And now I watch you working here. Why are you asking me?'

'It's just that...I've had an idea about you helping.'

'I'm a painter,' comes the instant, expected reply. 'I don't want to work with you.'

'No, no, I don't mean that. Listen, Rosa. There's a way you could really help the charities as a painter. I've been thinking this through for a while, and it's only an idea, but I'd like to propose it. You can say no.'

Rosa puts down her knife and fork. This man doesn't do things lightly. 'I've already refused your proposition of marriage, so I'd better hear you out. Tell me,' she says.

'Supposing you paint the stories of the work done by the charities?

You could create strong visual images and messages and stories that confront people head-on. It would be hard to turn away from a magnificent painting that depicts lives lived in appalling conditions, and ignore its message. It would be what we've been doing for years with our adverts and mail shots but on a much larger, more powerful scale. And you can paint in the good work done by the charity workers. The reality and the hope as well as the despair. Your paintings may be more persuasive in raising funds than all the words in the world. They could have a big impact.'

Rosa considers this new proposition. Is he intuitive, or does he just see her very clearly? His suggestion is remarkably timely because her grief for Henry has taken on softer hues and she feels ready to move in a new direction.

'How would it work?' she asks.

'Well, I'd go to some of the big companies and raise money both for your paintings and for the charities. It would work both ways. It would be good publicity for the charities and for the firms that finance the paintings. The companies will get kudos for their altruism and generosity.'

'Generosity they can well afford.'

'Well, yes, that's true, but it's a good use of their money, don't you think? They can also pay for a reception where your painting will be unveiled in the presence of some of the powerful and wealthy people who support the charity.'

'So I tell the story of the work done by a particular charity in a painting?' Rosa's imagination is fired up and she can see already how she can do this. She's thinking about the many portraits she'll need to include. And she's imagining compositions that pit good against evil, light against darkness. Yes, the idea is exciting.

'It would be a huge help. An excellent way of raising the charities' profiles. They are chronically short of funds.'

'I'd like to help,' she says, hearing all over again her parents' passionate commitment to helping the poor. Perhaps she sees this opportunity as a way of completing the circle they began so long ago. Yes, she likes the idea very much.

'Yes. I'm willing to try.'

Harold smiles his pleasure.

'Which charity first?' she asks.

'The Red Cross, the charity I'm working with now.'

'Do I just start?'

'No, no, my dear. We have to do it all correctly and in the right order. I'll introduce you and recommend you to the directors of the Red Cross.'

'I can't go myself?'

'No. Sorry. I need to smooth your way.'

'Oh, because I'm just a silly woman from Highgate who thinks she can paint!'

'I wouldn't put it like that, but we have to persuade them you are a serious painter and are doing this for the right reasons.'

'How ridiculous. Isn't it obvious? But all right, if we must.'

'Of course, the charity will pay for your travel and accommodation,' Harold continues. 'You won't be out of pocket.'

'Don't be ridiculous,' she replies. 'I'll pay for it myself. The press would love to twist that story. Imagine the headlines: Painter takes advantage of charity to fly around the world. Highgate lady sent on free holiday to view the sights. No! I'll finance everything myself.'

Harold is taken aback at her vehemence but knows when not to argue. Rosa's mind is made up. 'I insist I pay, Harold. It's the only way I'll take it on. I can afford it.'

'If you must.'

'I do. I agree to meet the Red Cross. I agree to fly out to India or Africa and see for myself the work that's being done. I agree to paint the scenes where the charity workers are making life more tolerable for the poor and the sick, and I agree to paint the portraits of the charity workers and the people they are helping. I don't agree to take any money for my fares or accommodation.'

Harold smiles and takes Rosa's hand.

'Thank you. This means a lot to me, and I hope it will be rewarding for you.'

*I'm glad I took that strong line. Many years later, after travelling round the world for The Salvation Army, a reporter said, 'By God, you're on to a good racket.'*

*'I paid my own fare,' I said, and that killed that scandalous story.*

Before leaving, Rosa buys herself a new camera. Harold raises an eyebrow.

'Branching out into another art form?' he asks her with a suppressed smile.

'Would you like to suggest another way for me to capture the likenesses of hundreds of people when I'm being whisked from place to place, country to country, and won't have time even to make sketches? And I doubt working people in India and Africa will have time to pose for me.'

'I take your point. But how do you feel about giving up the way you've been painting portraits for…how many years?

'Forty-five. Very excited,' she replies.

And so another door opens on Rosa's trajectory as an artist, in these, her later years of life. Already his companion, Rosa joins Harold Sumption in his fundraising work for charities and travels with him to see for herself the degrading and dangerous conditions in which people live and work. She comes home to paint, with compassion and truth, six by eight feet densely detailed storyboards. On each are hundreds of portraits of the people she met while she travelled – the charity workers, the farmers, the peasant women, families living in slums, young Indian widows destined for the funeral pyre, abandoned street children, the ill, the blind and the disabled. Rosa accurately paints their pain and suffering. As an artist, she translates hope into colour, light and beauty. Both dark and light will be brushed into a prodigious number of huge storyboard paintings which will help raise the profiles of many charities. For Rosa, this is a mission that she embraces with her heart and which will engross her for the next twenty years.

Today, Rosa is still painting charity storyboards.

*On the plane to Nairobi, I saw the sun rise through the clouds over the tops of mountains with that ethereal quality you find in the tropics. I was met by Lt Colonel Daniel Musasia and given refreshments before being taken to my hotel. My impression of Nairobi was of beautiful glass buildings and reddish roads with people asleep on the ground.*

*The more I meet The Salvation Army, the more I feel at home with them. Their faith in God gives them power to help people and to be happy themselves. Their life stories are so much more interesting than those of the Highgate middle classes whose lives are spiritually empty.*

*Harold Sumption.*
*http://sofii.org/article/the-father-of-modern-day-fundraising-harold-sumption*

# Nairobi
## 2000 [5]
## Age 67

Rosa is in the airport lounge, waiting to be called for her flight to Nairobi when she slits open a letter she hasn't yet had time to read. She had picked it up from the doormat and stuffed it in her pocket as she left the house and climbed into the taxi, letting the driver stack her pile of luggage that is heavy with drawing and sketching materials. The letter, she now reads, is from Haringey Council – an offer to provide her with transport so that she can get to the polling station and vote in the local elections. All of a few hundred yards down the road. She exhales an exasperated sigh. Ha! So in my sixties, I'm regarded as an old lady yet here I am about to travel alone to the five great continents to visit Kenya, Zimbabwe, Portugal, Switzerland, India, Hong Kong, Korea, Bolivia, Haiti and Dallas. Yes, I can list them all, in the correct sequence. I'm not losing my marbles yet. All the women in my family live to their nineties and I have every intention of doing the same. Help to get to the polling station? For heaven's sake!

The travelling from country to country might have been gruelling even for a younger woman, but Rosa takes it in her stride, supported by the charity workers who meet her and escort her to her accommodation, and buoyed up by seeing for herself lives that are very far removed, in every way, from those in Highgate. It's a huge learning curve but Rosa embraces it, seeing and storing an avalanche of material to take home to paint.

In Nairobi, she addresses a packed church congregation where the atmosphere is intense and breath-held, the singing strong and rhythmic. Rosa feels privileged to be the only white person present, and gives profuse thanks for the gift of an African skirt. Next stop is the first-ever

---

5. Rosa is delightfully vague about the dates of her trips to various parts of the world, so I have adopted the same attitude. The sequence is correct, as are the contents. The Salvation Army tour is recorded in detail, with precise dates, in *The Salvation Army*, July 2001, Vol 39 No 3.

home for street children who are taken out of a life of crime and taught carpentry, building and agricultural skills. Rosa bends down and talks to them, some so very young. They tell her they were abandoned as babies and survived in their street families. 'We were hungry, beaten and in constant danger,' they say. Rosa takes photographs, her heart bursting with sympathy. The following day she is driven along red dirt tracks through field after field of pineapples to a school for the blind where the children are learning braille. Again, she takes photos. She is told that only slowly are the charity workers managing to change the Masai belief that blindness is a curse causing the afflicted to hide themselves and to avoid the charity workers who come to find them with offers of help.

*This is the first time I have mixed in a serious way with black people without sensing tension. It has been a revelation to me. The Kenyans are fine, hospitable, loveable people.*


## Mumbai
## 2000
## Age 67

Rosa watches from the car window as she's driven to her lodgings and is appalled to see that the slums are worse than when she was last in Mumbai, and far worse than anywhere she saw in Africa. Lining every road are skin-and-bone people, rag-dressed people and barefoot children who sleep in doorways, exposed to the inclement elements while the monsoon is in full flood.

Although by now Rosa has seen all kinds of suffering in all kinds of places – after all, her purpose is to carry back the truth for her paintings – and she has learned to block unhelpful, overwhelming emotions, the following morning proves exceptionally harrowing and upsetting. Here, Rosa's protective shield fails. She is in the Booth Leprosy Hospital being introduced to patients with desperately severe disabilities, holding back her horror as well as her admiration for the bravery of the women, men and children with twisted, fingerless hands and missing legs. She takes photo after photo of their deformities while they tell her that every day they dip

heir hands in melted wax to try to soften their creased, withered skin. To
ıer surprise, the doctor tells her that they are quite proud of their disease
ɔecause it is a moneymaker. They beg during festivals and are given
nore money than those with other illnesses and disabilities. People feel
ı guilty pull to throw coins into their bowls because their deformities
ıre so very much on display and utterly shocking. Rosa, appalled at their
ɔlight, asks if leprosy hurts and is told by the doctor that they have no
ʿeeling in the affected areas and that pain comes only from infections
when the bacilli eat the cartilage between the toes and fingers so that
:he bones fall out. 'They can injure themselves easily because they feel
ıothing,' he says.

Her tour of the hospital continues into other areas and other rooms
where she sees hospital staff gently working with the invalids. One leper
is having his feet dressed and Rosa bends to take more close-up photos.
Then suddenly she feels the need to escape this almost unbearable
suffering. How would she cope with gnarled fingerless stumps for
hands? What would she do if she couldn't hold a paintbrush? The
thought sickens her but also shames her for it is not she who has to
suffer the deformities. She makes her excuses and leaves, taking herself
off through the plantation that belongs to the hospital and walks among
rubber trees, teak trees and coconut palms. The huge, shading leaves
soothe her. Pondering the plight of the invalids in the hospital, she feels
respect and admiration for the strength and care of the charity workers
who help them. In a way she doesn't need the photos because the images
are engraved in her head and in her heart.

Back in the peace and sanctuary of her rented house, she sits on the
verandah, listening to the croak of frogs and the call of birds, calming
her troubled soul. It is unbelievably beautiful. Her artist's eyes observe
that the monsoon has left a pale mistiness which has coloured the
contours of the land peach and apricot. She has already noted that in
these hot countries, when the sun shines, it knocks the colour out of
everything, but here, now, this place is pastel-tinted with an almost
luscious vegetation. There are palm trees and mango trees. There are
vines covered in peppercorns and flowers on the bushes. The colours are

magical.

The next day, Rosa travels on to Kerala. She's excited because Clive was here long ago and wrote to tell Noreen how beautiful it was. The India of fifty years past must have been indeed very fine without the pollution and noise of cars, Rosa thinks, but enough remains that is incredibly lovely. She thinks of her father here where she is now, thinks of herself following once again in his footsteps.

Late in the afternoon, having agreed to go to see a garden centre where they grow seedlings for teak trees, she finds herself hurtling through what looks like a jungle in a rusty old jeep with four scary men with flashing dark eyes and splendid moustaches who look more like guerrilla fighters than Salvation Army officers. The car sweeps through Indian villages with the horn blasting, scattering chickens and goats and ladies in saris.

Back in the five-star hotel in Trivandrum, Rosa sits on a cushion while fountains play around her. The sound of tumbling water goes some way to muffling the roar of traffic and the din of loud shouting, quarrelling and bartering outside. As night falls, she wants to leave and explore the town, but wonders if it would be unwise in case she is mugged. As a white woman she is too visible and too vulnerable. Still undecided, and chiding herself for being paranoid, she asks the opinion of the girl at the desk.

'Definitely don't go out alone,' the girl says, insistently shaking her head. 'There is a lot of crime out there. It's much too risky.'

'Thank you,' Rosa replies. And adds only to herself, 'The Salvation Army is taking such care of me, I suppose it's my job to make sure I arrive home in one piece.'

But the trouble with staying in hotels is a complete lack of exercise. Rosa is restless. She's taken to climbing the stairs to the fifth floor which is considered eccentric and charming by the staff. Young men in uniform keep appearing to offer to call the lift. Her host, Lt Col Abraham, is too busy coping with crises and has been late for both their meetings. That's good, Rosa tells herself. After two years of coming to terms with the loss of Harold, and throwing herself into work to keep her mind otherwise occupied, she feels herself finally unwinding and beginning to feel less old and tired. There is no need to run at life at full tilt. Not all the time.

Rosa's time here is drawing to a close and she slips the reel of film backwards through her fingers to find the best moments again – the palace made of wood where beautiful Indian girls with flowers in their hair got the giggles at the sight of a white woman; the walk through a village and paddy fields where Rosa took photos of cows bathing which she will use in the flood relief section of her painting; the drive into the mountains to see three impressive dams and a wonderful aqueduct. Everywhere, the poorest people in their faded, threadbare rags give her a warm welcome, making her think of exotic birds as they bend and bow, nod their heads and shuffle their bare feet. One of the villages is home to the untouchables. Cast out, the poorest of the poor, the most despised, they are visited by missionaries who tell them that they are loved by Jesus.

*This is a trip of contrasts. Yesterday I was visiting lepers. Today, a luxury hotel. I feel more at home with the lepers. Out of the window, I can see an old man begging on the street. The Indians believe it's his karma and he probably did something in another life to deserve his fate in this one. The doctor said the same about the lepers. With the help of The Salvation Army they will be reincarnated as princes. In the next life there will be an awful lot of princes!*

*We visited an orphanage for boys. I was introduced to a boy who was good at drawing. My heart went out to him, poor little soul, what a fate to be living in that place. Seeing him made me realise how lucky I have been all my life.*

**Haiti and home**
**2000**
**Age 67**

*I'm beginning to get very homesick. I'm longing to start painting again.*

But there is one more stop. Haiti. And the start of Rosa's stay on this remote island is far from propitious. Usually, when she emerges into the airport terminal, tired after a long plane journey but keen to begin collecting material for another charity painting in another country, she spots someone holding a card with her name on it. Someone comes forward to greet her, to make introductions, to make her welcome and reassure her that the practical arrangements for the rest of her stay are in others' capable hands. After a moment or two of anxiety, her eyes searching the crowd, the person with the card is a relief.

In the airport in Haiti, there is no-one standing still and holding up her name. Rosa has been travelling all day and is longing to hand herself over to an official from the charity who will take responsibility for whatever happens next. No-one comes up to her as she wanders round the airport, so obviously a woman alone who is expecting to be met. Soon she and other folk, the uncollected human luggage from the trip, are herded out to the courtyard and told to wait there because the airport gates are kept closed between planes to keep criminals out. It's hot outside with the sun on full beam. Half an hour passes. An hour. She remembers the passenger on the plane telling her that the country is a total shambles with a very high crime rate and that she will have to be forever vigilant. She is the only white person, the only woman waiting in the courtyard. Another half hour passes. Rosa paces the interior perimeter of steel railings, keeping her luggage in sight, aware that native men are watching her every move. They are eyeing me up to see if I'm worth robbing, she decides. Rosa, why aren't you more afraid? This is a really dangerous situation. As she paces, she ponders her lack of fear and decides that stoicism is in her genes, in the inherited characteristics of her ancestors who were army commanders who fought in vicious wars. However, as time passes, and the men continue to stare openly at her, she decides her best option is to pray. Rosa has never been religious, and praying is not something she turns to, yet now she sends up a heartfelt request: look, Jesus, you got me into this, you can jolly well get me out.

Maybe Jesus hears because a taxi driver approaches her, shows her his badge, and suggests that instead of standing in the blazing heat, she lets him drive her to wherever she wants to go. It's a risk, but without

the usual charity driver or officer, what else can she do? She gets in and shows him the only address she has – The Salvation Army headquarters. She doesn't know if this is where she is staying or whether it's simply the charity's base. The building sits in the midst of slum dwellings with high walls, steel gates and security guards. From a window, a worker sees the taxi stop outside, and rushes out to help her from the car and carry her bags, not knowing who on earth she is. When she explains, he and others who have gathered express horror that she waited so long alone and then climbed into a random taxi.

'You could have been raped, robbed and murdered,' one says.

'That's all right. Jesus was looking after it,' Rosa replies.

'He's not very reliable,' comes the quick reply.

It turns that out the fax and phone had stopped working, as happens frequently, and so they hadn't been informed that Rosa was on her way. They put together a makeshift meal of bread and peanut butter and Ovaltine, find her a bed, and then tell her she has arrived during the vacation when all their clinics are shut. The place is indeed a shambles.

The next day, the workers manage to get hold of Major Metelus and his wife, who are equally appalled at Rosa's unheralded and unmet arrival and rush to her rescue, taking her back to stay with them. At breakfast the next day, they tell her that under Papa Doc, their country had become violent and corrupt with terrible poverty. Similar to the Batista regime in Cuba, they explain.

As Rosa is taken to the obligatory church service, she sees for herself the abject poverty in which people here live. We in the West are so cushioned, she thinks. Here people are managing only to survive, and reach desperately for any hope. She notes that all the poor areas are littered with piles of plastic bags. Even the riverbed is stuffed with them.

This trip, unlike previous ones, is a bit of a letdown and Rosa starts to feel like a spare part as she's chauffeured to just a few select and safe places. While visiting an orphanage, she meets sixty-four-year-old Rosa Maria who came from an unhappy childhood to help the missionaries here, and who returns to Switzerland every year to raise money to build orphanages and schools in Haiti.

'Looks like I'm not going to see much of Haiti,' Rosa says to Rosa Marie. 'I've been to two church services and my hostess seems to sleep for most of the day.'

'The island can have that effect. I'm free for the rest of the day. I'll show you the island.'

A delighted Rosa is driven north and looks down on private beaches of white sand. The sea is the same turquoise as in the Caribbean, and on the horizon, fluffy clouds form silvery formations touched with gold. She wants to reach for a paintbrush to capture the colour and the light. Rosa Maria drives well off the beaten track, to the real, hidden Haiti, and everywhere they go, she is greeted with loving affection.

'I want to devote myself to children who are unwanted,' she tells Rosa. 'As I was unwanted myself.'

They continue on through banana plantations and sugar cane fields, before they come to an abrupt and unexpected halt where the bridge ahead has collapsed. Here they wait, while the traffic piles up, including lorries and buses carrying people crammed inside like sardines, hanging off the back, and sitting on the roofs.

'I'd be pretty fed up if I was stuck on one of those buses,' Rosa remarks.

'The people here are easygoing and accepting.'

'But we're all held up here and no-one is doing anything.'

Rosa Maria smiles. 'It's a battle to get anything done and nothing works. Patience!'

Finally a policeman arrives and all the traffic is diverted through banana plantations, on narrow, bumpy roads with the buses and lorries vying for pole position and overtaking at perilous speed. No passengers seem to fall off.

At the end of a long drive which reveals both the dramatic beauty of the place and its appalling infrastructure and chaos, the two women sit down to a meal in a restaurant on the coast. Rosa notes that the sea is cerulean blue with the sun sparkling in silver flashes.

*The round the world journey was life-changing for me. I'm not religious because I was brought up in the Communist Party and my husband used to say I was the most religious atheist he had ever met. I like the way The Salvation Army doesn't try to convert people but helps them sort out their problems.*

*When I returned from my world tour, it took me nine months to paint the picture. I had so many stories to include and lots of friends posed for me. The painting was unveiled at the Armourers' Hall by John Gowan in an event used for fundraising. The painting now hangs in The Salvation Army International Headquarters in Queen Victoria Street.*


## Mercy Ships
## 2007
## Age 74
## Unveiled in November 2008

*In London, you don't see much of it.*

While Rosa knows how to paint the sea, she regrettably doesn't get many opportunities to do so. Until, by a stroke of luck, she is introduced to a student whose parents are salmon farmers in Seattle. This couple come over to the UK to check up on their daughter and are so delighted to find her safe under Rosa's wing, learning classical techniques, that they invite Rosa back across the Atlantic to stay with them. It's timely, because Rosa has been planning to visit Mercy Ships as part of her research for a painting for The Rotary Foundation. It will be her fifteenth storyboard. She can combine work and pleasure, not that painting is ever work.

From Seattle, Rosa sails to Sitka, Alaska, to visit an unusual charity based on a ship. On the ten day crossing, she sits on deck, sketching the turbulence and contours of the waves, using her watercolors to replicate the exact colours of the sea as it shifts chameleon-like, under clear skies and glowering ones. The sea is deliciously capricious, ever-changing, ever-moving, elusive and mysterious. It's a fascinating challenge.

Mercy Ships was set up by two Americans, Don and Deyon Stephens, who were working as missionaries in Africa when their first baby was born disabled so they returned to Texas for medical treatment. Their experience brought home how hard it is to be poor and sick in third world countries. If people can't afford medical help, they are crippled or they die. Their first decision was to set up a hospital, but hostile tribes and violent criminals made the plan too risky a venture so they set up a hospital ship instead, an old-fashioned, out-of-service luxury liner which they kitted out with medical facilities. At the first hint of trouble or threat, they upped anchor and sailed away. Then they went public with a campaign to raise funds. They were gratified by the number of doctors and other medically qualified people who volunteered their help, paying their own fares and treating their stay on the ship as a working holiday.

Weeks ahead of putting into port, the Mercy Ship staff make sure that adverts are placed in local churches so people know they are on their way. When it docked in Sierra Leone, it was met on the quay by a queue a mile and a half long. People had walked from all over Africa with clubfeet, tumours, cataracts, infections and other problems they hoped and prayed could be treated with surgery.

Having seen for herself the fine care offered on the ship, Rosa flies out to Sierra Leone to be there for the opening of a new land-based clinic. Because of the very high birth rate amongst very young women in basic, primitive facilities, many develop complications, especially serious urinary tract infections, which require surgery. The operation is short but the girls need ten days afterwards in a hospital bed, and the ship was not coping with the numbers. A recovery clinic is needed to complement the ship's surgery. Rosa watches the unveiling of the building by the president of Sierra Leone.

After Sierra Leone, Rosa flies to Liberia at the time of the civil war and, for her own safety, is confined to the Mercy Ship with the medical

*Mercy Ships*

staff and patients. The country is a powder keg. She can go ashore only if a car is waiting with an escort of four UN peacekeepers including a bodyguard to escort her onwards. Everyone on the ship is under the constant protection of the UN. On board, Rosa hears rioting on the streets. Crime is dealt with instantly and brutally. The punishment for theft from a shop or the market, however petty, is death. Bodies are left piled on the pavements to set an example.

A female doctor asks Rosa if she'd like to watch an operation since her movements and activities are so very limited.

'Yes,' she replies. 'That will be interesting.'

'I'm going to remove a woman's eye,' the surgeon tells her. 'It's too infected to save. Is that something you'd like to see?'

'Of course,' Rosa says, and gets into scrubs ready for the operating theatre.

'Absolutely fascinating,' Rosa comments, as she leans in and closely watches the surgeon make the first incision. She's hugely impressed with the precision with which the doctor cuts through to the bone, changing blunt instruments for sharp ones and working with quiet concentration.

Rather like painting, Rosa thinks, watching rapt. The exactness. The correct sequence. One wrong move and you ruin the whole damn thing.

Throughout the procedure, the medical staff bat bad jokes round the operating theatre, while Rosa doesn't take her eyes off the cutting and scraping and stitching. The woman is wheeled away to have the wound bathed and dressed. As soon as the anaesthetic wears off, the patient sits up in her bed with a bandage covering her eye socket and thanks everyone warmly, including Rosa.

I can't remove an eye, but I can paint someone else doing it, she decides, and so another tiny piece of the jigsaw that is a charity painting is slotted into place.

*When I arrived back in Heathrow, I said to the taxi driver, 'Isn't it lovely to live in a country where there are no dead bodies lying around on the pavements?'*

*I told him where I'd been and about the Mercy Ships, and later he visited me in Highgate and saw my work. Three months later he was back to ask if I would do a painting for the London Taxi Benevolent Association For War Disabled.[6] After I had finished the Mercy Ships painting, I did that next. I always have a list and I always finish each painting in turn.*

*I have always loved working on a big scale and my training has enabled me to be able to paint anything. My thematic paintings for charity allow me to blend contemporary real issues with the techniques of the Renaissance painters. I feel I have found this amazing world and each time I paint one charity painting it leads to another.*

## United Way UK
## 2020
## Age 87

Rosa was right. One painting always leads to another by one means or another.

It was Rosa's daughter, Peggy Prendeville, who set in motion the wheels for the next charity painting. Peggy already had strong links with United Way UK, a national charity that supports local communities to ensure every family and every individual can reach their full potential through good education, financial stability and healthy lives. She donated one hundred and twenty of her children's books the previous year and visited the Berrymede Junior School in Acton where she read her book, *Manfred's Travels*, to four classes of delighted seven and eight year olds. Peggy was invited to an evening of musical storytelling with celebrated American pianist Gwendolyn Mok on the 15th November 2018 at the Princess Alexandra Hall of the Royal Over-Seas League. It was in support of United Way UK's Reading Oasis programme which donates entire libraries to under-resourced schools. Unknown to Peggy, they were going to talk about

---

6. In 2016, the charity's name was changed to The Taxi Charity For Military Veterans

her contribution to the charity in one of the speeches, but with tickets booked to a wedding in India, she was unable to attend.

Peggy writes: *I came up with the idea that my mum could paint a picture for them and therefore asked if she could go in my place so that she could meet them. I also asked if my two children, Isolde and Joel, could escort her as she wouldn't have known anybody there and I wanted her to enjoy the evening. Mind you, my mum has never been shy in coming forward (haha!) but I knew she would enjoy seeing her grandchildren too.*

An email was sent.

*My mother paints large 5ft x 8ft paintings for charities (and doesn't charge) and I wondered if you would be interested in her painting a picture for your charity. I've just told her about United Way and the Reading Oasis and she would love to paint a picture for you if you are interested - which you could then keep and use for publicity. Her charity paintings always tell the visual story of the charity which can include people who work for the charity too. Her first one was for the Red Cross (unveiled at Lancaster House) and then she went on to paint for thirty-one more for charities including Cancer Research, The Mercy Ships, four paintings for The Salvation Army, Help the Aged, Coram Children's Charity, Moorfields Eye Hospital, Barnardos and many more. She is also free tomorrow night and loves classical music so can she take our place at your event. I'm trying to get hold of my daughter, Isolde, to see if she can bring her so she doesn't get lost as she is 85!!*

Rosa readily agreed to paint for United Way UK after conversations at the concert and sso another huge painting telling the story of another charity started to take shape in her studio, layer by careful layer. It was finished in 2020.

And then Covid-19 herded us all into our homes and put an end to events and celebrations that would entice big crowds. United Way UK was unable to organise the unveiling of Rosa's latest painting.

We hope that by the time this book is published, perhaps in the late spring of 2021, there will be an unveiling of the United Way UK storyboard and it will be seen by all those who love and admire Rosa's work.

And we will give thanks to Rosa that she is still painting in her late eighties, even better that she considers these late paintings her best work.

Uniting communities

Bring health and happiness

encourage creativity

care for the old

Citizenship

Look after children

Education for all

Help eradicate poverty

Taking care of one another is the first responsibility of life

United Way

*United Way*

# Now

# I I  THE RECENT YEARS

# The recent years

## MBE
## 2010

*I*n *2010 I was invited to Buckingham Palace to receive the MBE from Prince Charles for my contribution to art and the charities. I remembered how Professor Coldstream from the Slade had warned me that copying in the National Gallery would ruin me as a contemporary painter. Sixty years later, I have had ten one-woman shows and have sold over four hundred paintings.*

## Honorary Doctorate
## 2013

In 2013 Rosa received an Honorary Doctorate from the University of Winchester.

*Rosa, Peggy and Michael.*

*Rosa receives her honorary doctorate*

# A tough year
## 2012
### From Rosa's personal memoir

'2012 was a tough year. My daughter's husband who had been with her for twenty-eight years, ran off with a Filipino artist. She kept phoning me in tears. I used the emotions I experienced in the Barnardo's painting – a portrait of my granddaughter running away.

At the same time, my son nearly died in hospital after surgery went wrong.

I was desperately worried about both children, even though they are grown up and have children of their own.

I was suffering from hip pain and after x-rays, I found out I had to have a hip replacement. I had it done and was very impressed with the result. I recovered in three months and it hasn't hurt since.

For about five years, I had been losing my sight and felt I was in a dense yellow fog. I was finding it more and more difficult to paint but I refused to give up. If I got very close to my subject and the canvas I could just see well enough. I had cataracts on both eyes, and had first one, then the other removed. It seemed like a miracle. After the first one was done, I could hardly believe the beauty of the colours I was seeing with one eye, while the other still saw yellow fog. I didn't give up painting during this time because I would have become very depressed and I won't allow myself to waste my life with depression.

There had been a lull in the charities coming to me because of the economic downturn. It was during this time that a professor at Winchester University, who had seen my work for The Salvation Army, asked me to do a painting for the new Winchester University. I went there and saw the modern building and big bare walls. I gave them the peacock painting and Jonah and the Whale and another of two people meeting in heaven.

Meanwhile Peggy has met a charming gentleman who has made her happy and Michael is well. The whole family is happy.'

*Rosa in the dining room*

# I am 84
## 10 March 2017
### From Rosa's personal memoir

'*Today I am eighty-four.*

*I am beginning to experience real old age. All my limbs ache, my eyesight is deteriorating and I feel tired a lot of the time. For the second time, I have slipped a disc in my back and apparently have a crushed vertebra due to osteoporosis.*

*The plus side is the experience I can fall back on. When people ask for a new painting, I seem to know how to do it. I've been asked to do a painting for the Samaritans and I immediately designed it in my head, deciding to show the contrast between happiness and misery. I'm going to Malta next week and will use the beauty with the sun rising over the sea. I'm getting more and more visions.*

*I am not painting to make money but to help and inspire people. Knowing this, when I paint, I forget my physical ailments because I'm concentrating on something more important and interesting. Thank God I'm an artist with an interesting life. If I can be brave and refuse to be oppressed by my ailments, this can be the most inspiring time of my life. With my experience and knowledge, I can create on a large scale the beauty and splendour of our world and the deeper dreams of my fellow human beings.*

*I'm a nutcase. I'm an automatic paintbrush.*'

# Appendix

## The technique of the Old Masters
## Taken from a telephone interview with Francesca Maxwell

https://rwa.org.uk/artists/francesca-berlingieri-maxwell

The technique is not taught much anymore except by a few colleges, perhaps Glasgow School of Art, and privately by some tutors. It's more than understanding the principles and the aesthetic of painting in this way, it's learning and experiencing the very physical, hands on, art and craft graft of rolling up your sleeves and getting your hands dirty, preparing the canvas and the pigments, mixing the right dilution and combination of different binders with the dry pigments which would have been ground to a fine powder by hand. Linseed oil and turpentine is used for oil paint, egg yolk for tempera, and honey for watercolour paint. It's too easy now to go to a shop and buy the exact colour from a tube, ignorant of the paints that were once made. Traditionally the canvas is linen stretched over a wooden frame then primed with gesso made from rabbit skin glue and whiting chalk. Many hours of practice would be spent on the drawing and the composition, then on the painting itself, handling the brush and layering the paint in thin layers, building up depths of colours and tones to create a rich and powerful representation of stories. This kind of painting is all-encompassing.

A whole generation has missed out on knowing how to paint this way. Long ago, students were apprenticed to painters and worked with them in their studios from a young age. An apprentice to an experienced etcher, for example, like Francesca Maxwell was from the age of fifteen, would work alongside the master, cleaning the copper and zinc sheets, preparing the paper and the inks in the old-fashioned, laborious way. They learned by observing and copying and practising, in their spare time studying and copying Old Masters in churches and galleries. They dedicated their lives to art. Students today are frustrated because they don't know *how* to paint a landscape or a portrait in the way they want. It's like having a vocabulary of fifty words and finding them completely inadequate for expressing their thoughts and feelings. Without the basic technique, they are missing the basic structure, language and tools.

Copying the Old Masters and learning the techniques they used is still taught in some countries such as China, Russia, The Netherlands and Italy. The UK and US broke away most fully, regarding the technique as too big a shackle and responsibility, and not wanting the enormous challenge. It went out of fashion as artists swung far in the other direction, perhaps feeling a desire to move on historically and break free from the past, perhaps daunted and intimidated by the prospect of even attempting to produce paintings in the style of da Vinci and Titian. Francesca Maxwell was taught when she was in her early teens, in an art school attached to the biggest art college in Italy, the Brera Academy in Milan. She was also taught, among other things, the principles of colour theory and composition based on the paintings of Kandinsky, Klee and Albers as well as the Gestalt principles of visual perception, art history and aesthetic.

## The layers

The technique used by the Old Masters is all to do with layers, building up a painting from the starting point of a complete if shadowy structure made with raw sienna, then adding colour starting with darker tones, and finally the highlighting and the details. The whole composition is seen in the very first layer. There is no hard and fast rule about the number of layers but layer is added to layer, and while the number of layers may vary, the order and progression is fixed.

First a linen or cotton canvas is stretched over the frame as the base to take the paint and primed with gesso.

1. The canvas is primed with a ground colour, usually a midtone. Renaissance painters used raw sienna, burnt umber or burnt sienna.

2. Drawing comes first, small or large, on paper. If the drawing is smaller than the size of the canvas, it is transferred to the canvas by squaring it and copying each part in each square. If it is the same size, the pouncing method is used: https://en.wikipedia.org/wiki/Pounce_(art)

3. Drawing on the canvas is made in charcoal. Excess charcoal powder is blown away and the drawing is fixed with a thin layer of painting, usually a slightly darker variation of the ground colour.

4. The painting is built up from the drawing with a series of washes which build tonality, and shape. Warm and cold tones are used to create volume and depth. The paint is diluted and used thinly, or dry brushing is used.

5. Lighter areas are painted over with more washes or dry brushing to add plasticity and luminosity.

6. Over the tonal painting, the colours are layered. Complementary contrasts and warm and cold colours in transparent or semi-transparent layers create vibrancy, texture, depth and contrast.

7. The lighter colours and highlights are added last using more dense and covering paint.

The brushstrokes and handling of the brush varies. Irregular organic lines can be used, feathering to create delicate transitions and dry brushing for texture. Lighter, softer application of the paint, wet on wet, is often used for hands and faces. The colour palette is kept to a minimum and all the colours are used across the painting over figures and ground to create a unified world. Paintings done this way were a visual storytelling and the artists would use all the tools at her/his disposal to produce a powerful, beautiful image.

# Praise for Lynn Michell's previous books

THE RED BEACH HUT

A compelling book that examines bigotry, ignorance, redemption and friendship. Beautifully told.

> – Heidi James, author of *Wounding*

Some of the best writing I've seen in a long time. The characterisation of Abbott and Neville is quite superb. .

> – Howard Sergeant, Writer and ghostwriter

RUN ALICE RUN

Run Alice Run traces the breaking points of a young girl's heart and the ways in which each fracture moulds her into the woman she's become.

> – Isabelle Coy-Dibley, The Contemporary Small Press

In this eloquent novel, Lynn Michell ultimately weaves a poignant tale of hard-won freedom.

> – Jenny Garrod, Dundee University Review of the Arts

WHITE LIES

A debut novel which possesses and is possessed by a rare authority of voice... It is the mother's voice that sings *White Lies* into unforgettability.

> – Tom Adair, *The Scotsman*

Gripping... with a bombshell of an ending.

> – Michele Hanson, *The Guardian*

LETTERS TO MY SEMI-DETACHED SON

A story of such painful intensity that tears poured down my face as I read it. No mother could fail to identify with her anguish and guilt, or her sense of failure.

> – Celia Dodd, *The Independent*

Moving, tersely written and painful to read. The honesty is remarkable.

> – Penelope Aspinall, *Event*

# Acknowledgements

I owe heartfelt thanks to:

– Rosa for telling me the story of her life and for trusting me to write her biography. It was a pleasure and a privilege to listen to her fascinating accounts of her childhood and student days, her marriages and relationships, and of course her passionate thoughts about art. As a woman and as a painter, she is an inspiration for creative women everywhere. I know from the feedback I have received that she is very much revered and very much loved.

– Heath Rosselli, Honorary Freeman of the Worshipful Company of Painter-Stainers and co-founder of The Worlington Movement for painters. Heath arrived like a fairy godmother late in the project and remained at my side while I navigated the final shallows of my journey. She was my go-between with Rosa and provided invaluable help with the artwork in the book. Her friendship is an extra, unexpected gift.
www.rosabransonandtheworlingtonmovement.com/
www.heathrosselli.co.uk/

– Michael Shpakov, Freeman of the Worshipful Company of Painter-Stainers, for giving me permission to use his uncannily recognisable portrait of Rosa on the book cover and for the many beautifully photographed illustrations inside the book.
www.michaelshpakov.co.uk/

– Martin Nicholls, Liveryman of the Worshipful Company of Painter-Stainers, for his generous organisation of the artwork for the book, his minute reading of the text and for his discussion of the Oxford comma.

– Sarah Cassidy for her intelligent, skilled, perfectionist editing of the text. She remained true to the structure and style of the book while she tracked down inconsistencies and mistakes with a forensic eye for detail. Unlike me, she is numerate as well as literate.

– Chania Fox, Emma McKay, Hannah McAuliffe and Sarah Hough, my superb Linen Press team, for their 11th hour proofreading and their constant, cheerful presence in the background, much valued during this last troubling and troubled year.

– Professor Joyce Goodman for proposing that we co-write a biography of Rosa Branson. That project faltered and split into two books. Goodman's book about art practices will follow.
www.winchester.ac.uk/about-us/leadership-and-governance/staff-directory/staff-profiles/goodman.php

– My gifted writer friend, Avril Joy, who has followed my seesaw progress with sterling patience. A lyrical author herself, she understands the intense emotions we invest in creating a book like this and, for its duration, how we ride the overlapping waves of self-doubt and elation.
www.avriljoy.com

Lightning Source UK Ltd.
Milton Keynes UK
UKHW020714220121
377503UK00007B/67

9 781838 060350